STRUCTURED
WALKTHROUGHS

STRUCTURED WALKTHROUGHS

Second Edition

Edward Yourdon

YOURDON inc.
1133 Avenue of the Americas
New York, NY 10036

© 1977, 1978 YOURDON inc.
1133 Avenue of the Americas
New York, New York 10036

Printed in the United States of America

ISBN Number: 0-917972-09-X

To my son,
Jamie Nash Yourdon,
who will always catch
the biggest fish.

CONTENTS

PART I: Introduction

PART II: The Mechanics of Walkthroughs

PART III: The Psychology of Walkthroughs

PART IV: Management's Role in Walkthroughs

ACKNOWLEDGMENT

A book on teams and walkthroughs should be written by a team and subjected to multiple walkthroughs. Unfortunately, this book wasn't; it is a personal work of art, in the most negative sense of the word.

However, this second edition has been improved enormously by the suggestions and criticisms of Lois Rose, P.J. Plauger, Tim Lister, Mark Krieger, Meilir Jones and Steve McMenamin who found a number of errors and weaknesses in the first edition, and suggested a number of improvements.

The second edition has also benefited from the careful hand of Toni Nash, who improved the punctuation and grammar, changed the format and layout of the book, and single-handedly produced the camera-ready copy for the printer. The book was set in Times Roman, using a Graphic Systems phototypesetter driven by a PDP-11/45 running under the UNIX operating system — but all the fancy hardware and software is useless unless someone with a practiced eye chooses the right type fonts, point sizes and formatting macros. Thanks, Sam!

And special thanks are due to Tom Plum. Many of the forms and procedures in this book are taken from technical reports and forms produced by Tom for use in our own company. Tom, far more than I, is the resident expert on programming teams and the group dynamics of walkthroughs — and this book is largely a reflection of the principles he espouses and puts into practice every day.

In the final analysis, though, this book is still a personal work of art. I anticipate several more walkthroughs and several more editions before all of my colleagues are willing to put their stamps of approval on it. In the meantime, friends, thanks for your help!

New York   Ed Yourdon
March 1978

STRUCTURED WALKTHROUGHS

PART I

INTRODUCTION

1 INTRODUCTION

This book is all about a modern-day phenomenon called *walkthroughs:* when to have them, how to conduct them, and how to avoid a variety of psychological problems that often accompany them.

But before we begin, there are several basic questions that need to be answered. What *is* a walkthrough? What do people hope to accomplish with walkthroughs? What can you hope to accomplish with this book? What assumptions does this book make about you?

All of these questions are answered in this chapter. If you are already familiar with the basic concept of walkthroughs, you can skip ahead to Chapter 2.

1.1 What is a walkthrough?

There is nothing mysterious about the basic concept of a walkthrough: It is simply a peer group review of any product. Throughout this book, we will assume that the "product" has something to do with a computer program or system; thus, we will be talking about walkthroughs of code, or flowcharts, or functional specifications.

As we will see in Chapter 2, walkthroughs can take place at various times in the development of a system. And a walkthrough can have various formats, and can involve various types of people. Despite the variations, though, the basic activity remains the same: a group of peers — people at roughly the same level in the organization — meet to review and discuss a product.

In your organization, and in articles you may have seen in the computer literature, walkthroughs may be referred to as code reviews, or design reviews, or inspections. They are also referred to as stompthroughs or structured walkovers, because of some of the problems we will discuss in Part III and Part IV of this book. In most cases, these other terms can be regarded as synonyms for walkthrough; in the few cases where different meanings are intended, we will give careful definitions.

1.2 Why do people practice walkthroughs?

To many programmers, the notion of spending an hour reading someone else's program makes no sense at all. And the thought of letting a group of programmers look at *their* code strikes them as a waste of time, if not an invasion of privacy. Why would anyone want to do such a thing? What is the point of structured walkthroughs?

The answer is very simple: *Walkthroughs are one of the most effective ways known to improve the quality of a computer program.*

For more and more programs these days, the most important measure of "quality" is *correctness*. It is embarrassing, expensive and sometimes disastrous to allow a large program or system to be put into production when it still contains bugs. Unfortunately, we are not yet able to generate mathematical proofs of correctness for any non-trivial "real-world" programs (and when we do generate such proofs, we have to worry about bugs in the proof!). And it is also evident that classical strategies of "exhaustive testing" fail to find all the bugs in today's complex on-line, real-time computer systems.

In contrast to this, walkthroughs have been found highly successful in producing reliable, bug-free programs; programming groups using walkthroughs report that they have been able to reduce the number of errors in production programs by as much as a *factor of ten*. In a typical organization, you can expect to find an average of 3-5 bugs in every *hundred* lines of code during the 5-10 year lifetime of a normal system. In systems developed with diligent walkthroughs, it is not uncommon to see as few as 3-5 bugs per *ten thousand* lines of code.

Of course, coding errors are only part of the picture. Many of our problems maintaining computer systems come from *design* flaws, or even worse, from errors in *analysis* or requirements definition. In some ways, such errors are far worse than bugs in the code: We can end up with a brilliant solution to the wrong problem. Obviously, walkthroughs can be extremely helpful in this area, too.

Not only does the walkthrough approach find *more* errors than classical development techniques, but it finds the errors more quickly and more economically. We will elaborate upon this point in subsequent chapters, but the basic reason is quite simple: The author of *any* product — and especially the author of a computer program — has a number of mental blocks which prevent her/him from seeing errors in his product as quickly as a group of peers. In addition, the walkthrough approach generally eliminates delays caused by slow turnaround for compilations, test shots, etc.

As a result of all this, most organizations find that walkthroughs increase the productivity of their development staff. This is not surprising, especially when we remember that roughly 50 percent of the time spent on most development projects is spent on testing.

In addition to detecting bugs, walkthroughs help increase the overall *quality* of computer programs and systems. In particular, walkthroughs can help spot gross inefficiencies in the design or implementation of a program; they can also help spot design strategies or coding techniques that would seriously detract from the maintainability of a program. It may not have been obvious to the author of a program that his/her method of accessing elements in a three-dimensional array would cause severe thrashing in a virtual memory environment; someone participating in a walkthrough will spot it. And it may not have occurred to the author that his/her choice of data names was cryptic, or even totally meaningless to others; a walkthrough will bring that out in the open.

There are other ways of ensuring the quality of a program; most organizations attempt to do this by establishing *standards* for the analysis, design, coding, testing and documentation of programs. While standards are certainly important, there are many situations where they have to be interpreted properly — so that the implementor obeys the *spirit* of the standards and not just the letter of the standards.

Unfortunately, the author of the program is not always in a good position to do this. For example, if the programming standards indicate that complex nested IF statements should be avoided, how can the author — whose ego is obviously involved — really determine whether *his* nested IF's are complex? The author's peers *can* determine whether the code is complex or not; they will react to it in the same way that a maintenance programmer eventually will. If they think the code obeys the spirit of the standards manual, then it's probably OK; if they don't think so, the fact that it obeys the letter of the standards is irrelevant.

Increasing the readability and the overall quality of computer programs can certainly be regarded as *tangible* benefits; on that basis alone, many organizations have enthusiastically endorsed the walkthrough approach. But there are intangible benefits as well: *training* and *insurance* are probably the two most important.

It doesn't require much imagination to see that a peer-group review can be an excellent way of communicating new ideas or advanced techniques to members of an EDP staff. Indeed, what is so surprising is that many programmers and analysts spend their entire career *without* any significant exchange of new ideas and techniques with their colleagues.

Naturally, we would expect that junior programmers would profit the most from a walkthrough approach, since they would have the opportunity to learn from the senior technicians. Sometimes, though, the opposite also happens: The senior people, who have gotten into a rut, learn refreshing new ways of approaching a problem from the junior people. This can sometimes be a source of embarrassment (a matter to which we will return in a later chapter), but it is normally quite beneficial for everyone concerned.

And finally, there is the insurance factor. In many development projects, an individual programmer/analyst's work is thrown away if he leaves before finishing his part of the project. Why? Simple: The new person who is given the task of taking over the incomplete work of the newly departed technician complains that it's disorganized, undocumented and thoroughly confusing. Clearly, it would be much faster to scrap the whole thing and start over . . . but not when the work has been subjected to several walkthroughs. In a walkthrough environment, several people would be familiar with the partially completed program; and the peer group would see to it that the work, though incomplete, was properly designed, properly documented and properly organized so that others could understand it. The result, in almost all cases, is that the work will not be lost — often with no loss of time — if the author has to leave the project before its completion.

As you can see, the advantages of walkthroughs are many: higher reliability, increased maintainability, better dissemination of technical information between technicians, and an increased likelihood that work can be salvaged if someone leaves the project. In Chapter 10, we will examine some statistics that quantify the effect of these benefits.

1.3 What will this book do for you?

This book has three objectives: The first is to acquaint you with the concept of walkthroughs, and the related concept of teams. In Chapter 2, we will discuss a number of different *types* of walkthroughs, and see where each type fits into a typical development life cycle for data processing projects. In Chapter 3, we will discuss the concept of programming teams — sometimes known as "egoless teams" — and their relationship with structured walkthroughs.

A second, and more important objective, is to provide you with guidelines and procedures for successful implementation of walkthroughs in your organization. Chapters 4 through 7 discuss roles of different people in a walkthrough, activities that should be carried out before a walkthrough takes place, the conduct of the walkthrough itself and the activities after the walkthrough.

A third objective of the book is to acquaint you with the psychological problems you are likely to encounter with other technicians, and with data processing management. Peer group reviews are not always as simple, friendly and objective as one would hope; and *programmers* are not always as rational, even-tempered and good-natured as one would hope. The situation is further complicated by EDP management, who are concerned about the impact that walkthroughs will have on their organization.

Chapters 8 and 9 are about the *psychology* of walkthroughs. These two chapters were written primarily for programmers, analysts and other technicians — but it certainly would not hurt managers to read these chapters to gain an appreciation of the problems that technicians face.

Conversely, Chapters 10 through 13 were written primarily for project managers — but it wouldn't hurt technicians to read the chapters. The more both groups understand about their respective roles, responsibilities and problems, the more likely that walkthroughs can be successfully implemented.

1.4 What assumptions does this book make about you?

The basic assumption that we make about you is that you have a reasonable amount of experience in the data processing field. While we will not dwell on the details of any particular vendor's hardware or any particular programming language, we assume that you are basically familiar with programming, systems design and systems analysis.

We also assume that you have been exposed to the basic concepts of structured programming, structured design and structured analysis. This is a fairly safe assumption, since walkthroughs have been introduced into many organizations as part of a "package" that includes structured programming, structured design, structured analysis, top-down implementation, chief programmer teams and a number of other modern systems development techniques. It's also a *necessary* assumption, because in many cases a walkthrough is only practical if the product has been developed in an orderly, comprehensible fashion — a proper walkthrough of a large, monolithic "rat's nest" program is almost impossible.

There is one final assumption: We assume that you are not the only person in your organization who is reading this book. After all, it doesn't make much sense having a walkthrough if only one person is involved. And, naturally, if your entire group is going to practice walkthroughs, they should all begin with the same vocabulary, the same concepts, the same procedures and the same ideas about how to avoid the "real-world" problems that will certainly come up.

It was with this in mind that the questions at the end of each chapter were developed. They are not intended to test your ability to memorize the contents of each chapter, but rather to stimulate discussion with your colleagues about issues for which the book does not — and cannot — provide a black-and-white answer. They are all *real* questions, and they have already been raised in many organizations. If you can't find anyone in your own organization who is willing to discuss them with you, write out your answers to the questions and send them to me at 1133 Avenue of the Americas, New York, New York 10036.

Questions for Review and Discussion

1. What are walkthroughs called in your organization? How do they differ from the walkthroughs discussed in this chapter?

2. Give some examples of walkthroughs or reviews in your organization *outside* the EDP department. How successful are they?

3. What are the objectives of a walkthrough? Can you think of any that were not mentioned in the chapter?

4. Do the programmers and analysts in your organization object to the idea of having their work reviewed by their peers? Do you? What is the nature of the objections? Do you think the objections are valid?

5. Does your organization keep statistics on the number of bugs found in production programs? How many of the bugs were caused by coding errors? How many were caused by design errors? How many were caused by analysis errors? Can you draw any conclusions about the relative importance of code walkthroughs versus design walkthroughs versus analysis walkthroughs?

6. How many bugs would you have to find before the investment of time in a walkthrough would be cost-effective?

7. How much of your organization's budget is spent on the maintenance of computer systems? What fraction of this do you estimate is caused by poor analysis, design and programming when the system was first developed? How much of this could be saved by having walkthroughs before the system is put into production?

8. Do you think walkthroughs would increase the productivity of the EDP staff? Why? By how much?

9. Does your organization have *standards* for the analysis, design and implementation of computer systems? If so, are the standards followed meticulously? At the present

time, how can your organization ensure that programmers are living up to the *spirit* of the standards and not just to the letter of the standards?

10. What procedures currently exist to train junior members of your EDP staff, and to upgrade the veteran members? Do you think walkthroughs would be a useful adjunct to these procedures? Why?

11. What are the chances that a partially completed program will have to be scrapped if the programmer has to leave the project suddenly? Do the programmers in your organization have the same opinion on this as management? Do you think walkthroughs would improve the chances of salvaging partially completed tasks?

12. Do you anticipate any other advantages of walkthroughs? What impact, for example, would it have on the overall morale of the EDP staff?

2 TYPES OF WALKTHROUGHS

2.1 Introduction

As we pointed out in Chapter 1, a walkthrough is simply a peer group review of some product. Thus, it is meaningful to talk about a walkthrough of *anything* by *anybody* at *any time*. For the purposes of this book, we are only interested in discussing walkthroughs of computer programs and systems; nevertheless, there is still an enormous amount of flexibility in the types of walkthroughs you may wish to conduct in your organization.

There are two major variables that largely determine the nature of the walkthrough. The first of these is formality: how organized, how "structured" should the walkthrough be? The second major variable is one of timing: At what stage in the development of a program should the walkthrough take place? As we will see in the remainder of this chapter, walkthroughs can take place after the specifications have been written, after the design has been completed, after the code has been written or after the test data has been developed — and in many organizations, walkthroughs are conducted at *each* of these milestones in the system development life cycle.

Indeed, walkthroughs can also be used *before* and *during* the development of specifications, design, code and test data. In addition to verifying the correctness and the quality of the finished product (whether specification, design or code), walkthroughs can also be profitably used to help *develop* the product.

2.2 How formal should a walkthrough be?

Unfortunately, many programmers and analysts have the impression that there can be only one kind of walkthrough. Some visualize the walkthrough as an impromptu "bull session" in which people gather around a blackboard to argue about some code that has been hastily scribbled in chalk. Others see it as a formal event, to which formal invitations are issued, and for which a formal presentation on overhead transparencies is required. Each group thinks that *only* its approach is a "true" walkthrough, and that one can have either a formal approach or an informal approach, but not both.

Nothing could be farther from the truth. It makes a great deal of sense to have *both* formal *and* informal walkthroughs, for each type has its advantages. And there can be "semi-formal" walkthroughs, where the participants decide for themselves just how formal and "structured" they will be.

Let's begin by discussing the *formal* walkthrough; after all, it's the type of walkthrough that is more commonly known in most organizations. It's often called a review, or design presentation, and it is intended to give reviewers a chance to offer formal approval or disapproval of the product. In many cases, the reviewers include the developer's boss — and *his* boss, and his boss's boss, and various other "big-wigs." And it may include total strangers from the Quality Control Department, the Standards Department, the user's organization and various others. In any case, it usually does *not* consist solely of the developer's peers, so it should probably not really be called a walkthrough.

What happens in such reviews? That obviously depends on the participants and on the product being reviewed. In some cases, the review is nothing more than a rubber stamp, since neither the boss, nor his boss, nor the person from Quality Control really understands what the design is all about. In other cases, it turns into an ugly political battle: The user complains that he never wanted the system in the first place, the Standards representative points out that the design violates every known standard in the organization, and the developer's boss blandly says that *he* had nothing to do with the design and that it's all the developer's fault. And sometimes — but only sometimes — the review turns out to be a frank, honest, productive exchange of ideas, suggestions and constructive criticisms about the product.

While it may not be entirely fair to generalize here, most of the "formal" reviews that we have seen were characterized by:

1.   A long preparation time: Formal invitations have to be issued, the review has to be scheduled to ensure that everyone can actually attend, and the producer has to spend a great deal of time developing notes, slides and flipcharts for his presentation.

2.   Slow feedback: The designer may have to wait weeks between formal reviews, only to find that his past week's work is judged unacceptable.

3.   Relatively complete and precise documentation to support the review — after all, the producer *has* to provide such documentation, in order to avoid embarrassing himself in front of his boss and all those other important people.

4.   Critiques whose quality is highly variable, depending on the competence, the mood and the attention span of those who attend.

5.   A general *absence* on the part of the reviewers of a sense of responsibility for the correctness and quality of the product being reviewed. The producer is usually viewed as being "stuck" with the product, and the reviewers have no real incentive to ensure that the product is of the highest possible standards before they approve it.

By contrast, the informal walkthrough can be held with relatively little preparation — it can consist of a few people looking at some scribblings on the back of an envelope. Consequently, the feedback from such walkthroughs is very quick — and the producer can often arrange to have several walkthroughs in the space of a day or two. Because the documentation *is* sometimes written on the back of an envelope, it tends to be much less precise — and as a result, many errors and flaws may be innocently overlooked by the reviewers. However, the overall quality of the review is likely to be better because the reviewers are peers of the author and presumably are somewhat familiar with the type of work he is doing; in any case, the quality of the review is likely to be more *consistent*. In addition, there is usually more of a sense of responsibility on the part of the producer's peers — after all, they have to work with him day after day.

Of course, there are times when informal walkthroughs are thoroughly superficial, and there are times when formal reviews are extremely productive. For a system of any reasonable size or complexity, we recommend *both* types of walkthroughs: informal walkthroughs to give the producer a chance to "bounce" ideas against his peers and see if there are any obvious problems; "semi-formal" reviews to look more carefully at the basic soundness of the design; and formal reviews to check carefully for subtle errors, design flaws and maintenance problems that may have been ignored in the excitement of creating the product.

2.3 When should a walkthrough be held?

In the previous section, we pointed out that a walkthrough could be either formal or informal — or any shade of "semi-formal." For obvious reasons, one tends to find that the informal reviews take place earlier in the development of a program or system, while the formal reviews take place later.

Let's illustrate this with one particular aspect of the development of a program: the coding phase. A code walkthrough could easily take place at any one of the following six stages:

- before the code is keypunched

- after the code is keypunched, but before it is compiled

- after the first compilation or assembly

- after the first "clean" compilation

- after the first test case has been executed successfully

- after the programmer thinks that *all* test cases have been executed successfully

There are advantages and disadvantages of having walkthroughs at these various points in time. For example, it is relatively unpleasant conducting a walkthrough when the source document is a coding sheet because (a) each reviewer probably has a nearly illegible reproduction of a coding sheet whose instructions were written in pencil, and (b) each sheet of paper probably contains only 10 or 20 lines of information, which means that the reviewer is constantly turning the pages back and forth to see what the program is doing, and (c) the reviewer sorely misses symbol tables, cross-reference listings, and other helpful aids normally produced by the compiler or assembler.

On the other hand, there are often tremendous delays associated with the keypunching and compiling of a program. If this is the case, the producers may wish to ensure that the code is correct before wasting a day (or as much as a week) waiting for it to be keypunched. It is for this same reason that some organizations conduct their walkthroughs after the code has been keypunched, but before it has been compiled — the source document is usually a simple "80-80" listing produced by an EAM machine.

It is *much* more common, though, to conduct a walkthrough *after* the program has been compiled. At that point, the reviewers are working with a more legible document, with more information on each page — and with the symbol tables, cross-reference listing, and other helpful information provided as a matter of course by the compiler. Some people argue that the walkthrough should not take place until the programmer has produced a clean compilation — i.e., one without syntax errors. In most cases, this makes sense *if* the data processing organization has reasonably good turnaround for compilations. Obviously, the developer must strike a balance here: On the one hand, he doesn't want to waste the time of his fellow reviewers looking for syntax errors that can be found easily by a compiler. On the other hand, he shouldn't spend several days submitting his program for compilation over and over again in an attempt to get rid of difficult syntax errors.

It is usually considered a bad idea to delay the walkthrough until the programmer has begun testing his program — and definitely a bad idea to wait until the programmer *thinks* he has finished *all* of this testing. First of all, a great deal of time has probably been wasted in this kind of approach: The programmer generally spends days beating his head against a wall, looking for his own bugs — when a group of reviewers would probably spot the bug much more quickly.

There are also some ego problems if the developer waits too long before having a walkthrough; we'll discuss ego problems in much more details in Chapter 9, but we can summarize some of the problems here. If one of the reviewers suggests that the code should be revised to make it more readable, the producer is likely to get quite defensive. After all, he's invested a great deal of time and energy — psychic energy as well as physical energy — and he's not terribly interested in suggestions about rewriting the program!

In addition, there is a psychological effect on the reviewers: One of the things that makes a walkthrough worthwhile for them is finding bugs. Indeed, many organizations argue that the more bugs that are found in a walkthrough, the more successful the walkthrough. On a personal level, a programmer probably won't mind spending an hour of his time reviewing someone else's code if he finds a bug or two. He feels that his time has been well invested. However, if he spends an hour reading through the code and does *not* find a bug . . . well, he begins to think that he's wasting his time. He begins to get sloppy, thinking to himself that there won't be any bugs in *any* code that he walks through.

The moral of all this is: You can have walkthroughs at any stage of the development of a product, but you'll usually find that it is less productive if you have the walkthrough too early or too late. You should schedule the walkthrough late enough so that the product is sufficiently well-developed and well-documented that some sense can be made of it — and yet early enough that (a) the producer doesn't invest too much of his ego in the product, and (b) the reviewers will have some bugs and improvements to find.

2.4 Types of walkthroughs

In the previous section, we discussed walkthroughs of one common aspect of a systems development project: code. Obviously, there are many other stages in the development of a typical computer system: analysis, design and testing are among the more obvious ones. Each of these activities can have — and should have — walkthroughs as well.

Specification walkthroughs are, as the name implies, a review of the functional requirements, or specifications, of a computer system. The walkthrough usually involves a systems analyst, a user representative and one or more designers on the project; its primary purpose is to spot problems, inaccuracies, ambiguities and omissions in the specification. The *document* that is reviewed in the walkthrough may be a narrative description of the proposed system, or a flowchart, or a data flow diagram, or a data dictionary, or any other suitable description of the requirements of the system.

Design walkthroughs assume that the functional requirements of the system have been correctly stated; the emphasis is instead on the *solution* to the problem. Design walkthroughs come in many flavors. One can imagine walkthroughs of

- A "logical" design, usually documented with a data flow diagram, HIPO diagram or structure chart.

- A "physical" design, often documented with a system flowchart or other appropriate document. In a large system, one would find many different walkthroughs of different aspects of the physical design — e.g., walkthroughs of the data base design, walkthroughs of the design of the telecommunications subsystem, walkthroughs of the backup/recovery subsystem.

- a "procedural" design — i.e., the low-level flowchart or pseudocode of the logic within individual modules. Such a design would immediately precede the actual writing of code for the module.

Code walkthroughs often attract the most attention in organizations — simply because they weren't done before. The product being reviewed is, quite simply, the code, e.g., a program listing. Unfortunately, code walkthroughs sometimes uncover analysis problems or design problems (usually because the preceding walkthroughs were ignored or performed in a superficial manner), to the dismay of the programmer who spent days writing brilliant code.

Test walkthroughs are conducted to ensure the adequacy of the test data for the system — *not* to examine the output from the test run. Attendees at such a walkthrough would typically include the person who developed the test data, other programmers (including, probably, the author of the program*), a systems analyst, and perhaps a user representative if he can be enticed to join in the fun.

It should be pointed out that a number of other people can make a useful contribution to *all* of the types of walkthroughs mentioned above. Auditors, Quality Assurance representatives, EDP Operations personnel, representatives of EDP standards organizations, and others can help point out serious problems *before* the system is "in production." In many organizations, such problems are discovered after it is too late: The user cannot afford to have the system taken out of production, and the development staff has already moved on to another project.

---

* Note the strong implication here that the author of the program should *not* be the one who develops the test data.

Questions for Review and Discussion

1. Discuss the characteristics of *formal* reviews in your organization. Who attends? How quickly can they be set up? How thorough is the review? How much of the review consists of "politics"?

2. What are the characteristics of an informal walkthrough?

3. Do you think formal walkthroughs and informal walkthroughs can co-exist in your organization? What procedures should there be for determining when a product is ready for a formal review?

4. For a code walkthrough, when do you think the walkthrough should be held — e.g., before the code has been keypunched, after it has been compiled, etc. How much of this depends on the *environment* in which your programs are developed? For example, would your opinion be different if every programmer had his own terminal, with access to a fast time-sharing system?

5. Some people argue that even if computer time is cheap and easily available, it is far better to find bugs *before* the program has been entered into the computer? Do you agree?

6. Can you think of any additional types of walkthroughs besides the ones listed in Section 2.4 of this chapter? What about documentation walkthroughs? Conversion walkthroughs? Installation walkthroughs?

3 PROGRAMMING TEAMS

Before we proceed further with our discussion of walk-throughs, we need to briefly discuss the related topic of *programming teams*. The original idea of walkthroughs was largely suggested by Gerald Weinberg in his classic book, *The Psychology of Computer Programming* (Van Nostrand, 1971). Indeed, whenever you hear discussions about walkthroughs, you are likely to hear such phrases as egoless programming, programming teams, democratic teams, adaptive teams, and even programming families. While your organization may never implement the concept of programming teams, it's a good idea to understand what they are.

3.1 Background of teams

In many industrial organizations, and in many social organizations, the value of *teams* has been recognized for hundreds — even thousands — of years. In the last few years, for example, several automobile companies have experimented with the idea of production teams that are responsible for complete production of whole subsystems of a car. As an alternative to the traditional assembly line approach, the team approach has generally led to higher productivity, lower absenteeism, higher quality products, and improved employee morale. The team normally arranges its own daily work assignments, and even handles its own minor disputes and discipline problems — all of which is usually "invisible" to management outside the team, which is concerned primarily with the overall productivity and quality of the work.

As another example, consider the teamwork normally found in championship football, baseball and basketball teams. While individual players may make the headlines because of a spectacular play or a streak of outstanding performances, the team depends on the talents of *all* of its members for long-term success. Indeed, there are many instances of a team losing a game in spite of the outstanding performance of one of its members.

We could spend a considerable amount of time discussing the psychology and management of such teams, but that is not really our purpose in this book. The main thing that you should see is that the notion of a team of cooperative peers, whose minute-to-minute activities are usually decided *without* the intervention of management, is not such a new and radical idea.

3.2 A brief look at classical EDP organizations

Now compare the structure and dynamics of the teams mentioned above with that of the classical EDP organization. In most such organizations, a manager — often with the title of project leader or lead programmer — determines the work assignments and gives individual programming tasks to the programmers. If the project is a smashing success, it is usually the manager who gets the largest share of glory; if the project fails or falls behind schedule, it is also the project manager who bears the brunt of the criticism from higher levels of management. This means that the programmers themselves often feel no real responsibility (other than their own private compulsions) to make the project a success; in particular, they generally have no incentive to share their programs with their peers, or to invest any significant amount of energy to help their colleagues find bugs in their code.

Indeed, the situation is often even more cold-blooded. In many organizations, the programmers know that there is a limited amount of money available at the end of the year for salary increases; alternatively, they may know that there are one or two "slots" available for promotion to higher grades within the organization. If there are ten programmers in the organization, and only two slots for promotion, it follows that there is a certain amount of competition between one programmer and another. Or, to put it another way, each programmer feels that if he spends too much time helping his colleague, it will detract from his own chances of getting a raise or a promotion.

In such an environment, it is extremely common for each programmer to develop an ego attachment to his programs — indeed, he usually refers to them as *his* programs, his personal property. (It's interesting to note a similar possessiveness in certain assembly line workers, and in certain administrative workers who are trying to make some sense out of an inhuman job.) At the very least, the programmer is defensive about his code, and is reluctant to accept any suggestions or constructive criticisms from other programmers; in the extreme case, he may hide his listings and refuse to show the programs to anyone else.

3.3 Objectives of programming teams

An environment of the sort mentioned above sounds pretty grim . . . and maybe it is a bit extreme. Unfortunately, a number of large programming shops — e.g., banks, insurance companies and government agencies with upwards of a thousand programmers under one roof — are beginning to behave more and more like this. As you might expect, programming teams are an attempt to create a more human, more productive programming environment.

The purpose of teams in the programming field is primarily to change programming from "private art to public practice," as Harlan Mills puts it. Or, to use Weinberg's words, the intention is to change programs from "private works of art to corporate assets." That is, instead of creating an environment where programmers work *alone* throughout their career, we create, with programming teams, an environment in which everyone feels free to discuss and critique everyone else's programs. Why? Primarily because the team is organized so that its members have a common goal, and so that each member can expect similar rewards if the project succeeds, and similar penalties if the project fails (just as in a baseball team, where the whole team suffers if one person strikes out at a critical point).

One of the benefits of the team approach is that it can take advantage of the talents of different members at different stages in the project. Just as a baseball team depends critically on good pitching at certain points in the game, good fielding at other stages, and strong hitting at still others, so a programming team finds it needs varying degrees of expertise in analysis, design, programming, testing and debugging at various stages of the project. And some people are good at design, but unimpressive when it comes to the "dirty work" of actually grinding out the code; others are very unimaginative at the design stage, but are work horses who can produce phenomenal amounts of code once the design has been sketched out. Some have a talent for generating test cases to thoroughly shake down a system, while others are best at the mysterious art of debugging: They can read a 500-page hexadecimal dump and actually "see" bugs lurking among the hexadecimal digits. Forced to work on their own, each of these people will excel in one or two stages of their assignment, and will do a mediocre job at every other stage; working together as a team, they can take advantage of critical talents when and where they are needed.

Chances are that you've already seen examples — albeit informal examples — of teams in your data processing career. One of the best examples of this is in the *training* of EDP personnel: Compare the environment in a typical university programming course with the environment in a typical training program in industry. In the university, each student is expected to compete: After all, there are only a few 'A' and 'B' grades to be given out. And if the instructor finds that you've been helping one of your fellow students get his program working, he's likely to flunk both of you! In industry, on the other hand, the basic object is to make *everyone* succeed in the difficult task of learning to program: After all, the organization has invested a substantial amount of time and money in the fledgling programmer, and it is uneconomical to set things up so that people fail if they don't have to. At the same time, the training budget in most EDP organizations is so small that the instructor often doesn't have enough time to give adequate personal attention to each student — so he simply tells the students that they should use some kind of "buddy system" to help each other out. In most such train-

ing programs, you'll find groups of two or three trainee programmers huddled around a dump, trying to figure out why one of
them is having a problem. In the end, they *all* learn from the
process, and they *all* win. And so does the organization . . .
until it decides to put them into a "real" programming assignment, where programmer-to-programmer competition and the
other political realities of modern corporate life usually destroy
any tendencies towards teamwork that the new programmer may
have had.

3.4 How a team functions

To some, this description of programming teams sounds
highly radical — indeed, almost communistic. In practice, it is
rarely anything of the sort: Members of a typical programming
team are law-abiding, reasonable human beings who look, act
and think just like anyone else.

In fact, many organizations have programming teams
without even *knowing* that they have teams. The most common
example of this is a typical development project where the
manager is inexperienced, uninterested or incompetent to provide strong leadership — and where the technicians gradually
discover that they have common ideas and interests in the design
and implementation of their system. In such a case, the technicians may be unaware that they are actually operating as a team,
and management may be equally ignorant of the situation.

In organizations where teams have become a formal concept, it is still common to see a *project* used as the justification
for forming a team. The team is given an assignment, with appropriate constraints (budget, schedule, etc.), and is then given
considerable freedom to develop its own day-to-day operating
procedures. The critical thing, as we have said, is that the team
operates in an environment where all of the team members feel
free to discuss and critique each other's work. This discussion of
other people's programs is usually formalized in the *walkthrough*
approach which is the primary subject of discussion in this book.

3.5 Problems with teams

We have implied in the comments above that programming teams are not all that common, nor are they all that popular. Indeed, the notion of programming teams does run counter to the classical way of organizing programmers on a project. Why? What kind of problems should one expect in a programming team?

One aspect of the true programming team is that nobody is really "in charge" — nobody is the boss, in the traditional sense. This generally makes outside management somewhat nervous ("Whose rear end are we going to kick if the project comes in behind schedule?"), although that problem sometimes can be circumvented by nominating one team member as the spokesperson for the group. The absence of a formal boss may also be difficult for some team members to handle — a number of people are accustomed to, and would prefer, an authoritarian manager to tell them what to do.

Note also that the typical programming team probably doesn't have any "superprogrammers" — if it did, we would probably call it a "chief programmer team," in keeping with terminology introduced by IBM. However, most companies don't have any superprogrammers anyway — so maybe the programming team is the best way to cope with the large number of average programmers a company employs.

Obviously, the mere act of putting three or four people into a project does not make them function automatically as a *team*. Implicit in the concept of a team is the notion of working closely together, reading each other's code, sharing responsibilities, getting to know each other's idiosyncrasies (both on a technical and a personal level), and accepting a *group* responsibility for the product. If this attitude *can* be instilled, the effect is usually one of synergism: Five people working together on a team may produce twice as much as they would working individually.

We should make one other comparison between the chief programmer team and the "egoless" team. *If* you have a superprogrammer in your organization, the chances are that *he's* not egoless — he's very good, and he's happy to tell everyone just how good he is. This may well destroy the democratic aspect of the team — especially when it comes to walkthroughs. You may find that the superprogrammer (or chief programmer) wants to review all of the code *by himself*, rather than making it a group activity — and that sort of one-on-one confrontation between an individual programmer and the superprogrammer is hardly likely to be egoless.

There are many who feel that programming teams are the wave of the future. In organizations where the concept has been successfully implemented, the results have been quite impressive — and the programmers will generally say that they would never revert to their "old" way of doing things. On the other hand, many organizations have found that they simply cannot implement the concept: there are too many psychological problems, too many personality clashes, and too many political problems.

In summary, then, it seems that the concept of true programming "teams," or "families," will probably be implemented in only a small number of relatively progressive EDP organizations. But if that's the case, why are we talking about them? The reason is very simple: About the only aspect of the team concept that is likely to be implemented is that of a walkthrough. Keep that in mind. Walkthroughs approximate team programming and are one of the first steps towards establishing programming teams.

Questions for Review and Discussion

1. Has everyone in your organization read *The Psychology of Computer Programming?* If not, why not?

2. Give some examples of teams outside the EDP field. Can you see anything they would have in common with programming teams?

3. In your organization, do programmers, designers and analysts openly compete with each other for raises and promotions? If so, does it have any noticeable impact on the way EDP systems are developed in your organization? What impact does it have on morale?

4. Is it common for the programmers in your organization to feel possessive about their programs? What attitude does EDP management have towards this ego attachment?

5. What do *you* think the objectives of a programming team should be?

6. Do you think that programming teams will work in your organization? Is it likely that everyone will receive a similar reward if the project is successful? Do you think teams could exist without the tacit approval of EDP management?

7. What problems would you anticipate if programming teams were formed in your organization? How difficult would the problems be to solve?

8. Do you think that walkthroughs can be successfully implemented in an organization that does *not* endorse the concept of programming teams? Why (or why not)?

PART II

THE MECHANICS
OF
WALKTHROUGHS

4 ROLES IN A WALKTHROUGH

4.1 Introduction

A successful walkthrough involves several people, each of whom plays a definite role. The roles need not be permanent: one person can be a coordinator in one walkthrough, and a secretary/scribe in the next. Indeed, it is possible for one person to play more than one role in a single walkthrough.

The important thing is to recognize what the important roles are, so that you make sure that they are properly played in the walkthrough. In subsequent sections of this chapter, we will examine each role in turn. We will mention only briefly the specific *duties* to be carried out by the people playing these roles; the details of those duties will be discussed more thoroughly in Chapters 5, 6 and 7.

4.2 The presenter

The most obvious role is that of the *presenter.* That is, a typical walkthrough involves at least one person whose task is to present the product — the design or the code, for example — to the rest of the group. We will see in Chapters 5, 6 and 7 that the presenter has important activities to carry out *before* the walkthrough takes place, *during* the walkthrough and *after* the walkthrough.

In most cases, the presenter is also the *producer,* or *author* of the product being reviewed. This makes obvious sense: It is the producer who most wants to know if there are any problems with his design or code; it is the producer who will have to fix any flaws or bugs that are detected in the walkthrough; and it is the producer who, since he knows his product, is in the best position to present it to the others.

However, some people argue that for just this reason, the producer should *not* be the presenter: There is an excellent chance that the producer will brainwash the reviewers into believing that the product works just as he, the producer, thinks it does — and as a result, the reviewers may overlook certain flaws and bugs. To avoid this problem, many organizations ask that the product be presented by someone other than the author; it may be a "buddy" of the author, or it might even be someone who was not directly involved in any aspect of the development of the product.

We can carry this one step further: In some walkthroughs, there may not be a need for a presenter. If the product is sufficiently self-explanatory, the reviewers should be able to study the appropriate documentation (e.g., program listings, HIPO diagrams, etc.) on their own, and then attend a walkthrough to discuss their criticisms and suggestions.

For the remainder of this book, we will assume that the walkthrough *does* involve a presenter. Local circumstances will usually determine whether or not this is really necessary — and the rest of the walkthrough approach works the same regardless of whether or not there is a presenter.

4.3 The coordinator

The next role — and perhaps the most important — is that of the *coordinator*. As the name implies, the coordinator ensures that the activities of the walkthrough are properly planned and organized. As we will see in the next three chapters, the coordinator plays a crucial role before and after the walkthrough, ensuring that everyone is properly advised of the walkthrough, and properly prepared.

During the walkthrough, the coordinator serves as a moderator, and ensures that the discussion does not stray from the subject at hand. Consequently, it is often suggested that the coordinator should be the team leader, project manager, chief programmer or some other "senior" person. While this can be done, we advise against it; Chapter 11 will elaborate on the reasons for avoiding a "heavy" management presence in the walkthrough.

4.4 The secretary/scribe

Another important role is that of the *scribe,* or the *secretary.* As the name implies, this person takes notes during the walkthrough; the notes serve as a permanent record of the results of the walkthrough, and are critically important if the walkthrough is to be used for ongoing quality assurance of the product.

It is often suggested that the scribe can be a "clerical" secretary — i.e., someone who is good at taking shorthand, good at typing, but probably unfamiliar with any of the details of programming, systems design or other technical aspects of the product. This usually turns out to be a mistake: Since the reviewers' comments are often made quickly and in rather cryptic terms, the scribe needs to be someone who can take notes rapidly without having to interrupt the walkthrough for definitions and clarifications. In addition, the scribe needs to know which reviewer comments can be ignored, and which need to be written down — we *don't* want a verbatim transcript of the walkthrough, but rather an intelligent summary of the bugs that were found, the suggestions that were made, and the questions that were raised. Consequently, we suggest that the scribe should be a participating member of the team, if the team approach discussed in Chapter 3 is used; in any case, it should be a person who is familiar with the technical details of the product being reviewed.

One other point should be made here: The scribe will usually be so busy taking notes that he will be unable to actively participate in the discussion of the product. Consequently, if the scribe also wishes to play a role as a reviewer, it is probably best that he review the product individually *before* the walkthrough, and summarize his comments in writing. Alternatively, the role of scribe could be rotated from person to person, so that no one person gets stuck with the job too often.

4.5 The maintenance oracle

The roles that we have discussed thus far have not been of a *reviewing* nature; instead, they were concerned with the presentation and administration of the walkthrough. Obviously, a walkthrough has to have reviewers as well; however, it is important to recognize that different *types* of reviewers are necessary.

One such type of reviewer is a person we'll call the *maintenance oracle*. His role is an obvious one: to review the product from the viewpoint of future maintenance. The reason we use the term "oracle" is that the reviewer must try to look into the future, to anticipate what kind of change might have to be made to the product. For example, the maintenance oracle should ask himself whether the product is essentially "self-documenting," and whether it could be maintained if the producer were no longer in the organization.

In many organizations, the maintenance oracle is a person who does not work in the same group that is producing the product. For example, the maintenance oracle may be a member of a quality assurance department, or a member of the maintenance department. In many cases, the quality assurance department or maintenance department will have to look at the product sooner or later anyway — and by including such a person in a walkthrough at an early stage of development of the product, many nasty confrontations can be avoided later.

4.6 The standards bearer

Another important role is that of the *standards bearer*. As the name implies, the person who plays this role is primarily concerned with adherence to standards — programming standards, design standards, or any other kind of standards that the organization follows. One of the reasons that this is an important rule is that standards need to be interpreted in an "intelligent" fashion: Obeying the letter of the standards is not as important as obeying the spirit of the standards. By including a standards bearer in the walkthrough, comments can be made from the viewpoint of someone who is presumably defending the standards; and counter-comments can be (and often are) made by those who feel that a strict interpretation of the standards is not warranted for the product under consideration.

We often find that the standards bearer and the maintenance oracle come from the same department in an organization; indeed, they may be the same person.

4.7 A user representative

Where appropriate, the walkthrough should also include a *user representative,* i.e., someone who can ensure that the product is meeting the customer's needs. Among other things, this helps avoid the unfortunate phenomenon of creating a brilliant solution for the wrong problem.

In most organizations, the user — or a user representative — participates in the earlier walkthroughs of a product. For example, the user could be expected to play a major role in a specification walkthrough, and possibly a design walkthrough. He probably would not participate in a code walkthrough, but he could definitely play a constructive role in a test walkthrough.

4.8 Other reviewers

A typical walkthrough will include one or more additional reviewers whose primary interest is to give a "general" opinion of the correctness and the quality of the product. Such reviewers usually work in the same team or the same project as the producer, though that is not necessarily the case; indeed, it is sometimes extremely useful to include one or more reviewers from outside the immediate group. The outsider can often bring a fresh, objective perspective to the product, while the "insiders" may be so close to the product that they miss some obvious flaws.

4.9 Who chooses the reviewers?

In the previous sections, we have identified several useful roles in a walkthrough. That leaves us with one major question: Who decides which people should attend the walkthrough? That is, who decides whether it is important to have a maintenance oracle, for example, and who decides whether a user representative should be invited to attend?

The answer is: It depends. Depending on the project organization, either the producer will decide who should attend the walkthrough, or the project manager will decide, or the *team* will decide.

In a team environment — of the sort discussed in Chapter 3 — we assume that the entire team is responsible for the correctness and quality of the final product. In that case, all of the members of the team should attend the walkthrough — and the team should decide whether additional "outsiders" should be invited.

In a typical non-team environment, each programmer or analyst is usually held personally responsible for the correctness and quality of his own product; consequently, the producer invites whomever he wants. If he deliberately avoids inviting important people — such as the standards bearer — it is he who will eventually suffer. On the other hand, if there are reviewers with whom the producer simply cannot get along, he has the freedom to avoid inviting them.

In an organization where management plays a more active role, the project manager or team leader may decide who should attend. And for the more formal reviews, there may even be organizational standards that dictate who should attend.

There is a basic point to be made here: Several of these approaches to selecting the reviewers can co-exist in the same project. At the earlier stages of a product, the producer may wish to invite only one or two people of his own choosing — just to have a "quick-and-dirty" walkthrough to see if there are any major flaws in the product. As the product becomes more and more finalized, the walkthroughs may become more and more formalized — and the selection of reviewers may be increasingly outside the producer's control.

There is one last aspect of walkthroughs to discuss at this point: How many people should attend? As we have seen from the previous discussion, there are at least six distinct roles that can be identified. Of course, some roles may be combined — and in some walkthroughs, it may not be necessary to include certain roles. In any case, most organizations find that 5-6 people is enough for a good walkthrough, and that more than 5-6 becomes unproductive. Conversely, a walkthrough can be held by as few as two people (the producer and one reviewer), and will often involve only 3-4 people. The fewer people that participate in the walkthrough, the more likely that certain bugs and flaws will be overlooked; the more people that participate (above 5-6), the more likely the walkthrough will degenerate into a committee meeting.

Questions for Review and Discussion

1. Do you think the producer should present his own product in a walkthrough? What are the advantages and disadvantages of such an approach?

2. How easy do you think it would be for the producer to "brainwash" the reviewers into believing, as he does, that his program is correct? Can you cite an example of this?

3. Do you think it's possible for a walkthrough to take place without *any* formal presentations of the product? Under what conditions would this make sense? What are the advantages and disadvantages?

4. Do you think that the coordinator should be a project leader or some kind of management representative? What are your reasons? Does your management agree with you?

5. Do you think that the scribe *must* be a programmer? Could the scribe be a clerical secretary? Could the scribe be the "program librarian" found in many chief programmer team organizations?

6. Should the maintenance oracle be a member of the same group that is building the product, or should he be an outsider? How is this handled in your organization?

7. How strong a voice should the standards bearer have in the walkthrough? Should he be left out of the early, informal walkthroughs until the product has begun to be finalized? What is the opinion of the standards people in your organization?

8. How many walkthroughs do you think a user should attend? What do the users in your organization think of walkthroughs?

9. What kind of additional participants could play a constructive role in a walkthrough?

10. Who do you think should determine the makeup of the re-
    viewing audience — the producer, management, or the pro-
    gramming team? Why? Does it always have to be done
    the same way?

11. How many people do you think should attend the walk-
    through? Do you think there should be a minimum and
    maximum number of attendees?

5 ACTIVITIES BEFORE THE WALKTHROUGH

5.1 Introduction

As we saw in Chapters 1 and 2, there are many variations on the basic walkthrough format. One area where there is a great deal of variety is the amount of preparation that takes place before the walkthrough. At one extreme is the programmer who dashes off the last line of code, leaps on top of his desk, and yells to the entire office, "Anybody here wanna have a walkthrough?" At the other extreme is the programmer who treats the walkthrough as if it were a black-tie affair, to which he issues formal, engraved invitations.

Obviously, neither extreme is desirable. But it is a theme of this chapter that a certain amount of preliminary organization and preparation is necessary in order to make the walkthrough as effective and as productive as possible. The primary reason for this is that the walkthrough involves the time of half a dozen highly paid people. Their time should not be wasted; indeed, the walkthrough should be run as if every minute is precious.

Of course, there is only one way to make the walkthrough move smoothly and briskly: planning and preparation ahead of time. This chapter discusses these preparations by reviewing the activities of the producer, the coordinator and the participants.

5.2 Responsibilities of the producer

Obviously, it is the producer who initiates the walkthrough. While his responsibilities are obvious and almost mechanical, they are crucial if the walkthrough is to succeed at all.

The producer's first responsibility is to announce his intention to have a walkthrough. This should be be done at least two days in advance, so that the participants will have adequate time to do their preparation. If the producer is certain that the participants have ample spare time, the walkthrough can be announced one day in advance, or even one hour in advance. However, most EDP organizations are far too hectic to allow for such last-minute planning: It will almost always turn out that an important participant is out of the office, that another is in a meeting (or in another walkthrough!), and yet another is engaged in a critical project that can't be interrupted for a day or two.

The producer's second responsibility is to choose a coordinator and participants for the walkthrough. As we discussed in Chapter 4, some organizations may take this out of the producer's hands: The entire team may attend the walkthrough as a standard practice, or the project manager may decide who should attend. But it is common for the producer to decide who would be most appropriate to review his program or his system design.

The producer is also responsible for providing appropriate documents for the walkthrough: listings, HIPO diagrams, specifications, etc. These are usually given to the coordinator, who arranges for their distribution to the other participants.

This raises an interesting point: What should the producer do to occupy his time during the two days before the walkthrough? In most organizations, this is not a problem: The producer has other programs to write, other projects to work on — even other walkthroughs to attend. If he is concerned that he might *not* have anything to do, the producer could announce his walkthrough a day or two *before* he has actually finished his product. The major problem with this is that he probably won't have any documents ready for distribution; consequently, the reviewers will be forced to attend the walkthrough "cold," and the quality of the walkthrough will suffer accordingly.

It is not easy to make a choice between a producer who may spend an idle two days waiting for the walkthrough, and a group of reviewers who may be wasting their time reviewing a product they have never seen before. The best possible solution is the one in which the producer (and the reviewers) can break their work into small tasks, each of which can be worked on individually. It is worth noting in passing that a project developed using top-down structured analysis, design and programming has the advantage of breaking a system into small, highly independent modules, each of which can be worked on separately by one or more analyst/programmers.

The producer has one final responsibility: to choose a product that *can* be reviewed in a period of 30-60 minutes. This necessarily limits the scope and size of the product: One can expect to walk through 50-100 lines of code, 1-3 pages of a HIPO diagram or structure chart, or 5-10 pages of a written specification. Obviously, if the producer is developing a *large* product, the walkthroughs have to be done one piece at a time; once again, a top-down structured approach makes this easy to accomplish since it organizes a system into a hierarchy of modules, each of which can be reviewed independently.

5.3 Responsibilities of the coordinator

The coordinator has important responsibilities before, during and after the walkthrough. The most important of these is to ensure that the walkthrough actually *will* take place; his other responsibilities ensure that the walkthrough will run smoothly and effectively.

Once the coordinator has been chosen by the producer, he selects a specific time and place acceptable to all the reviewers. This may involve reserving a conference room or some other meeting place. In any case, it requires the coordinator to contact each of the other participants to choose a mutually convenient time and place.

This brings up the second responsibility of the coordinator: to ensure that the participants will actually attend. In most cases, this simply means that the coordinator has to personally contact each of the participants and confirm that they will be available for the walkthrough — *and* that they have have the time (and the interest) to devote an hour to reviewing the producer's documentation before the walkthrough. Depending on the situation, the coordinator may have to play the role of "mother hen," coaxing, nagging and chiding the participants to attend the walkthrough.

There is one last responsibility: The coordinator has to take responsibility for distributing the documentation associated with the walkthrough. This usually involves the reproduction of several pages of material, as well as its distribution to the participants.

5.4 Responsibilities of the participants

Finally, we come to the participants. Their primary responsibility is simply to agree to *be* participants, and to contribute the necessary time and energy to make the walkthrough successful. While this is an obvious point, it needs to be emphasized: *if a participant feels that he will be unable to devote enough time to review the product, it is better that he not participate, rather than performing a superficial review.*

How much time is necessary? That depends on the nature of the product being reviewed, and on the participant's general familiarity with the product. In most cases, the participant should expect to spend approximately one hour reviewing the documentation for a walkthrough that will last 30-60 minutes.

Of course, there may be situations where a participant feels somewhat unfamiliar with the product being reviewed — or where he has questions about some details of the program, the design or the specification. In such a situation, the participant should plan on spending as much time as necessary *before* the walkthrough with the producer — and the producer should be prepared to devote as much time as necessary to familiarize the participants with his product.

How can the participant be sure that he has devoted enough time to a walkthrough? And how can the coordinator — and, most of all, the producer — be assured that the walkthrough will not degenerate into a superficial "rubber-stamp" approval of the product? One useful rule is this: Each participant should bring to the walkthrough at least one negative comment and one positive comment about the product being reviewed. Though this may seem a simple-minded rule, our experience has been that it works: Each participant feels compelled — through peer pressure, if nothing else — to make at least one or two intelligent comments about the product.

Questions for Review and Discussion

1. Why is it important that preparations be made before the walkthrough begins?

2. How many days in advance do *you* think a walkthrough should be scheduled? Do you agree with the suggestion of two days? What are your reasons?

3. What do you think the producer should be doing during the two days before a walkthrough takes place? In your organization, is it easy to find other things to do while you're waiting?

4. What is the maximum size product that can be adequately reviewed in 30-60 minutes? How many lines of code? How much of a HIPO diagram or structure chart? How many pages of a specification?

5. What are the responsibilities of the coordinator before the walkthrough?

6. How can the coordinator ensure that the participants will invest the necessary time and energy to study the documentation before the walkthrough takes place?

7. What should be done if an invited participant fails to attend a walkthrough without a reasonable excuse? Should he be shot? Should he not be invited to subsequent walkthroughs? Is this something that the programmer should decide for themselves, or is it something that should be left up to management?

8. How much time do *you* think needs to be spent before the walkthrough in order to properly acquaint yourself with a product that is to be reviewed?

6 ACTIVITIES DURING THE WALKTHROUGH

6.1 Introduction

Finally! After five chapters of introduction, we come to the walkthrough itself. You may think that this chapter will be almost anticlimactic at this point, but the long introduction has been necessary — and it parallels the long buildup before a *real* walkthrough. The objective, as we have pointed out in previous chapters, is to provide as much advance preparation as possible, so that the walkthrough will proceed as quickly and efficiently as possible.

It is important that all this preparation not be wasted once the walkthrough begins. The discussion and activities in the walkthrough proper should be organized and methodical (hence the name *structured* walkthroughs) so it will not degenerate into an aimless argument between two programmers.

There are two rules that *must* be observed during the walkthrough proper if it is to be successful. First, everyone must agree to follow the same set of rules and procedures — just as a convention or congress agrees to follow Robert's Rules of Order. Second, the participants must agree and understand that it is the *product* that is being reviewed, not the *producer*.

Continuing on the theme of the previous chapters, we will discuss the major activities of the walkthrough in terms of the primary participants. Once this has been accomplished, we will discuss a number of additional guidelines for successful walkthroughs.

6.2 Roles and responsibilities in the walkthrough

The *coordinator* begins the walkthrough by calling the assembled group to order. Though it is usually unnecessary, he may wish to remind the group of the nature and purpose of the walkthrough: In an organization that is carrying out walkthroughs of a number of different products, it is not unusual to see someone accidentally show up at the wrong meeting!

The *producer* then takes the floor. If this is the *first* walkthrough of his product, he will usually begin with a general overview of the program or design. Following that, he will present his product — whether it is a program listing, a HIPO diagram or a specification — piece by piece, making sure that every piece is reviewed.

From the discussion in the previous chapters, we can see that there may be several variations on this approach. For example:

1. If the reviewers have had ample opportunity to study the documentation before the walkthrough, then the producer's initial presentation can be kept mercifully brief.

2. The reviewers may be concerned that the producer will "brainwash" them into making the same assumptions about the product that he did; consequently, they may prefer that he make *no* initial presentation. This approach is also taken in organizations where the reviewers wish to ensure that the product is "self-documenting," for the sake of future maintenance.

3. If he is unsure, the producer may simply ask the reviewers whether they consider it necessary to provide an overview of his document.

4. In some cases, the producer may wish to enlighten the reviewers as to the background of the product: alternative approaches that were considered, trade-offs that were taken into account, assumptions that were

made, etc. One could argue that all of this should be included in the documentation provided to the reviewers before the walkthrough — but it is unlikely that it actually will be.

If this is the second (or subsequent) walkthrough of his product, the reviewer should begin by reviewing "old business" from the previous walkthrough. In most cases, this will involve a point-by-point discussion of the bugs, suggestions and comments raised in the previous walkthrough. For example, the producer might say, "You'll see as we walk through this program that I fixed the bug that Fred found in the GLOP module; you'll also notice that I followed Alice's suggestion to rewrite the nested IF's in the FOO module. And I did some research into Charlie's suggestion that we make the ZARK routine recursive; unfortunately, it increases the run time by a factor of ten, so I decided to stick with the original approach." To do this, of course, requires that both the producer and the reviewers have a detailed list of the comments that were raised in the previous walkthrough; this list is provided by the scribe, whose responsibilities are described below.

The *reviewers* have an obvious responsibility in the walkthrough: to make constructive criticisms, comments and suggestions. To avoid wasting time, the reviewers should give the producer *(and* the scribe) a list of errors that require no explanation — e.g., syntax errors in a program listing or spelling errors in a specification. Each reviewer then presents his comments about the product — making sure that his comments are directed at the product, rather than the producer.

Naturally, the producer will be tempted to argue about some of the comments, or defend his product, or challenge some of the assumptions made by the reviewers. As much as humanly possible, this should be avoided: For one thing, it tends to consume a lot of time, and for another, it raises the possibility of nasty ego confrontations. A basic principle to keep in mind is: *The basic purpose of the walkthrough is error DETECTION, not error CORRECTION.* Thus, the producer should not respond to any of the reviewer's comments in the walkthrough, except to ask that the reviewer's comments be clarified — he should *not* argue about the validity of the reviewer's comments. *After* the walkthrough is over, the producer will have ample time to review the suggestions in a more dispassionate mood, and (if necessary) find one of the reviewers for a private discussion or argument about comments raised in the walkthrough.

Throughout the walkthrough, the scribe takes notes on the comments made by the reviewers. Figure 6.1 shows a typical walkthrough report form, and Figure 6.2 shows a typical completed form. Note that the comments are recorded in summary form; the scribe does not have the time for long, verbose comments — nor should the reviewers need such verbosity.

When the walkthrough has finished (i.e., each of the reviewers has had a chance to make his comments), the coordinator should ask the group for their recommendations concerning the product that has been reviewed. There are normally three possible recommendations:

- The group may vote to accept the product in its present form.

- The group may vote to accept the product with the revisions suggested in the walkthrough. This implies that they trust the producer to make the revisions correctly.

- The group may vote that another walkthrough is necessary — either because a substantial number of errors were found (and the group is concerned that the correction of the errors may introduce new errors), or because some controversial suggestions and criticisms were raised.

Should the vote be unanimous? Should it be a simple majority vote? Should it be a non-enforceable record of the opinion of the reviewers? That depends on the nature of the organization: In a programming team environment, the team assumes responsibility for the correctness and quality of the work of any of its members — so the vote would have to be unanimous. In a more loosely structured "semi-team," a majority vote might be sufficient. In an organization where the reviewer assumes total responsibility for his product, the reviewers should merely offer their opinions — and the producer should then decide whether additional walkthroughs are necessary.

6.3 Additional guidelines

By now, you should be able to conduct a successful walkthrough. However, that doesn't necessarily mean that it will be entirely trouble-free. In subsequent chapters, we will discuss personality problems and psychological problems which can ruin an otherwise successful walkthrough; for the remainder of this chapter, we will discuss a number of guidelines that can help avoid the more mundane problems encountered in a walkthrough.

1. *Keep the walkthroughs short.* Walkthroughs are mentally fatiguing, and the reviewers cannot expect to maintain their concentration for more than an hour, or two hours at the *very* most. Try to keep the walkthroughs to 30 minutes, if possible — indeed, there's nothing wrong with a 15-minute walkthrough. Among other things, you'll find that the reviewers will be more willing to participate if they know it will be brief; the coordinator will also find it easier to arrange the logistics for a short walkthrough. But the most important benefit is the increased concentration, which almost certainly leads to a better review of the product. People sometimes forget that there's nothing magic about a walkthrough: It takes hard work to find bugs, and the bugs are not likely to leap out of the program listing if the reviewers are daydreaming about baseball or sex.

2. *Don't schedule more than two consecutive walkthroughs.* This suggestion follows from the previous comments. One can expect the first walkthrough to be very productive, the second acceptable. By the third walkthrough, the reviewers are mentally exhausted, and by the fourth, they're sound asleep (mentally, if not

Figure 6.1
A Sample Walkthrough Form

Co-ordinator
Project

Co-ordinator's checklist:

1. Confirm with producer(s) that material is ready and stable _____

2. Issue invitations, assign responsibilities, distribute materials

   Date _____ Time _____ Duration _____

   Place _____

Responsibilities	Participants	Can attend?	Received materials?
_____ _____	_____	_____	_____
_____ _____	_____	_____	_____
_____ _____	_____	_____	_____
_____ _____	_____	_____	_____
_____ _____	_____	_____	_____

Agenda:

___ 1. All participants agree to follow the (same!) set of rules.

___ 2. New project: walk-through of material

   Old project: item-by-item checkoff of previous action list

___ 3. Creation of new action list (contributions by each participant)

___ 4. Group decision

___ 5. Deliver copy of this form to project management.

Decision: ___ Accept product as-is
          ___ Revise (no further walkthrough)
          ___ Revise and schedule another walkthrough

Signatures		

Figure 6.2
A Completed Walkthrough Form

INSTALLED 3/29/77

YOURDON

MEMORANDUM

To: _____   Date: MAR 24 77

From: Co-ordinator: _____   Subject: Walkthrough of:
                                        first

A. Announcement of meeting; RSVP

    Date: Mar 28 (mon)   Place: Plum's office

    Time: 1 Pm   Duration : 15 min

Participants	Responsibilities	Can attend?	Received materials?
✓ Plum	Co-ord Sec'y		
TDP	Specs		
Nate	Users		
Tom R	Standards		

B. Distribution of materials (at least two days prior to walkthrough)

    Attached are the materials for the walkthrough; please bring your
    marked-up copies and written notes to the walkthrough.

C. Agenda for the walkthrough:

    ___ 1.   All participants agree to rules in Form SW-2 (Tech Report 3)
    ___ 2a.   New project: walkthrough of material
    ___ 2b.   Old project: item-by-item checkoff of previous action list
    ___ 3.   Creation of new action list (contributions by each participant)
    ___ 4.   Group decision
    ___ 5.   Deliver copy of this form to project management.

D. Decision

    ✓ Accept product as-is
    ___ Revise (no further walkthrough)
    ___ Revise and schedule another walkthrough

E. Signatures of walkthrough participants

physically). Even if the walkthroughs are as short as 15 minutes, mentally "switching gears" from one topic to another makes it difficult to have more than two consecutive walkthroughs. A one-hour break is usually sufficient for everyone to revive his brain, and get ready for another round of walkthroughs.

3. *Don't walk through "fragments" of a product.* Though this suggestion should be obvious, we have observed a number of EDP professionals attempting to walk through a 50-statement fragment of an unfinished program, or the first three pages of a detailed specification. In most cases, this occurs because the producer felt obliged to meet a deadline for the walkthrough, regardless of whether he was ready for it. From the reviewers' viewpoint, the walkthrough serves very little purpose; the frustration they feel at reaching the end of the fragment of the product can only be compared to *coitus interruptus.* The moral: review *complete* pieces of a product — i.e., the specification, or the design, or the code for an entire module or program or system.

4. *Use standards to avoid disagreements over style.* Despite the admonitions earlier in this chapter, it is common for arguments to break out between the reviewers — or, more likely, between the reviewers and the producer. Sometimes the argument will revolve around a bug — e.g., whether or not the program really is operating correctly or doing what the user wants it to do. However, many of the arguments concern *style:* Reviewers may disagree about the use of GOTO statements in a program, or they may criticize the graphic conventions used in a HIPO diagram. The producer has two problems with this: First, he may sincerely feel that his style is appropriate (particularly if he has considered several alternatives privately before coming to the walkthrough); second, the psychological and emotional commitment to his product makes it difficult to scrap it and begin anew.

Though we will return to the psychological problems in later chapters, there is a *procedural* approach that will often avoid the nastier conflicts over style and format: *standards*. The very word "standards" usually sends a shiver up the spine of the average EDP professional, for he feels that a 17-volume tome on standards has no relevance to his day-to-day work. Thus, it is ironic that several organizations have begun to see standards in a whole new light — as a way of avoiding fistfights in the walkthrough.

In most cases, the reviewers do not need to use the entire 17 volumes of "official" standards; indeed, it is far more common for the group to extract the few pages that apply to their product, or to make up their own "ad hoc" standards. The ad hoc standards are usually only a few pages long, and they can be developed using the same walkthrough approach as for other products.

Of course, it would be time-consuming and expensive to develop a set of standards for each new product being reviewed. However, it makes a great deal of sense to develop a common set of standards for all of the analysts, designers and programmers working on a common EDP project.

5.   *Let the coordinator maintain decorum in the walkthrough.* When a group of intelligent, articulate, aggressive EDP people get together for a walkthrough, it is easy for things to get out of hand. Indeed, things can get out of hand even if the participants are unintelligent, inarticulate and basically passive — EDP people just seem to have a natural talent for arguing! And in the midst of their arguments, they may be reluctant to heed the coordinator's plea to maintain order and decorum — especially if the coordinator is a peer without the authority to *order* the participants to shut their mouths.

The only way the group can avoid the risk of turning the walkthrough into a noisy brawl is to agree ahead of time that they *will* respect the coordinator's role — and that they *will* stop arguing if the coordinator asks them to. If this cannot be done, one of two things will eventually happen: (a) the walkthroughs will be perceived by everyone as unproductive and will be abandoned, or (b) management will insist that a project leader play the role of coordinator — i.e., the coordinator will become someone who *can* order the participants to shut up.

Questions for Review and Discussion

1. What are the two most important rules for ensuring the success of a walkthrough?

2. Do you think that the producer should begin a walkthrough by presenting his product to the reviewers? What are the advantages and disadvantages?

3. Are there any situations where the producer definitely should *not* present his product to the reviewers?

4. Why should the producer not argue about the criticisms and suggestions raised by the other reviewers?

5. What recommendations can the reviewers make at the end of the walkthrough? Can you think of any in addition to the three mentioned in this chapter?

6. Should the reviewers' recommendation be based on a unanimous vote, or can it be the result of a simple majority?

7. Why should walkthroughs be kept to 30-60 minutes? Is there anything wrong with a walkthrough that is significantly shorter than 30 minutes — e.g., 5-10 minutes?

8. How many consecutive walkthroughs do you think can be held before the quality of the walkthrough deteriorates?

9. How can standards be used to avoid arguments over the "style" of the product? Are there any other ways to avoid such arguments?

7 ACTIVITIES AFTER THE WALKTHROUGH

7.1 Introduction

This will be a very brief chapter. Indeed, you might wonder why we need a chapter at all: What is there to say about a walkthrough *after* the walkthrough is over?

That's just the point. A lot of people think that nothing remains to be done after the walkthrough is over. As a result, a number of small, but nevertheless important, loose ends are not properly taken care of. Hence this chapter, to emphasize those few details that need to be done to properly finish off the walkthrough.

As in the previous chapters, we will discuss these post-walkthrough activities by outlining the responsibilities of the various participants.

7.2 Responsibilities of the coordinator

The coordinator has the most important "clean-up" activities. He breaks the walkthrough report that we saw in Figure 6.1 into two distinct pieces: a management summary, and a set of detailed comments made by the participants.

The management summary, shown in Figure 7.1, is normally delivered to the project manager or to the person who is responsible for monitoring progress of the product that was reviewed in the walkthrough. Note that the management summary does *not* indicate how many bugs were found, nor does it reveal the detailed comments and criticisms that were made by

Figure 7.1
The Management Summary

Co-ordinator

Project

Co-ordinator's checklist:

1. Confirm with producer(s) that material is ready and stable _____

2. Issue invitations, assign responsibilities, distribute materials

    Date _____ Time _____ Duration _____

    Place _____

Responsibilities	Participants	Can attend?	Received materials?
_____	_____	_____	_____
_____	_____	_____	_____
_____	_____	_____	_____
_____	_____	_____	_____

Agenda:

  ___ 1. All participants agree to follow the (same!) set of rules.

  ___ 2. New project: walk-through of material

        Old project: item-by-item checkoff of previous action list

  ___ 3. Creation of new action list (contributions by each participant)

  ___ 4. Group decision

  ___ 5. Deliver copy of this form to project management.

Decision: ___ Accept product as-is
          ___ Revise (no further walkthrough)
          ___ Revise and schedule another walkthrough

Signatures		

the reviewers. Instead, it simply states *what* was reviewed, *when* the walkthrough took place, *who* attended the walkthrough and what the verdict was. This is usually more than sufficient to give management an adequate feeling for the status of the product.

As for the detailed comments made by the reviewers, it is generally agreed that management wouldn't understand them and wouldn't be interested in them. In any case, we feel that management shouldn't see the detailed comments — for once it becomes known that management *does* look at the detailed comments, the objectivity of the walkthrough is threatened. We will have much more to say about this in subsequent chapters.

The detailed comments should be filed, in case they are needed at some point in the future. Most organizations feel that the detailed comments, *plus* a copy of the management summary, should be filed along with the "official" copy of the documentation itself — i.e., along with the official program listing, the HIPO diagram or the specifications. In many projects, this documentation would be maintained by a project librarian (or a program librarian, if the chief programmer team organization is used), so the coordinator would simply turn over the detailed notes to the librarian.

Finally, the coordinator has the responsibility for delivering a copy of the detailed comments to each of the participants. This should be done as quickly as possible — i.e., within an hour after the walkthrough is over — so the participants can review it while the details are still relatively fresh in their minds.

Once all of this has been done, the coordinator can turn himself into a toad and vanish.

7.3 Responsibilities of the participants

The responsibilities of the participants depend largely on the producer. In most cases, the participants have nothing to do — other than to review the copy of the detailed comments given to them by the coordinator to ensure that there are no errors.

However, there will be occasions when the producer wishes to discuss some detailed points that were not fully resolved in the walkthrough itself. If, for example, the participant commented in the walkthrough that he felt that 16 levels of nested IF statements were difficult to understand, he might find that the producer wanted some help in figuring out an alternative, more reasonable, approach. And if the participant found a subtle bug in the walkthrough, there's a good chance that a *solution* to the bug was not offered in the walkthrough. Thus, the participant may find that the producer approaches him after the walkthrough, asking for help in fixing the bug.

While the participant technically has no obligation to help the producer solve his problems, we feel that he has a moral obligation to spend up to an hour explaining in detail the comments and criticisms that he made in the walkthrough. This is particularly true if the participant's comment was of the form, "I disagree with the *style* of this product because . . ." or "My opinion is . . ."

Of course, it is possible that the producer may try to get the participant to solve *all* of the problems raised in the walkthrough. It is important that the participant remember that the *producer* is the one who "owns" the problem — unless the product is being developed by a true programming team (of the sort discussed in Chapter 3), in which case they *all* own the problem. In a conventional EDP organization, though, it is perfectly appropriate for the participant to say, "Hey, Charlie Producer, I'd be happy to brainstorm with you for an hour or so, but I've got a lot of other work I've got to finish this afternoon. I'm afraid you're gonna have to go off in a corner and figure this out for yourself."

7.4 Responsibilities of the producer

Finally, the producer: What responsibilities does he have? From the comments above, we can see that his primary responsibility is to ensure that he *understands* the comments, criticisms and suggestions that were made during the walkthrough and that have been documented in the walkthrough report. He doesn't have to agree with all of the comments — and he doesn't have to have solutions for all of the problems that were pointed out. But he should at least understand what everyone was saying. If he doesn't, he should have the opportunity — and the responsibility — to pester the participants until he *does* understand.

What then? In the final analysis, we have to assume that the producer probably knows more about the product than the participants — so he's the one who will have to decide which suggestions can be easily accommodated and which ones are impractical. Thus, the producer should seriously and objectively consider each suggestion, each criticism and each complaint — and accept those suggestions which seem appropriate, compromise where it seems reasonable, and reject those suggestions which turn out to be unreasonable. Of course, if his product was rejected by the reviewers, he has to take into account that the same suggestions and criticisms may well be raised on a subsequent walkthrough; consequently, the producer may decide to accept some suggestions even though he doesn't completely agree with them. And if he strongly disagrees with the suggestions, he has to be able to come up with a rational argument that he can present in the next walkthrough.

The very last thing the producer must do (assuming that the product was not completely accepted) is to start the cycle all over again; that is, he has to decide when he's ready for another walkthrough. As we've pointed out, the next walkthrough will typically begin with a review of "old business," so the producer needs to be able to show — either in the product itself, in the accompanying documentation or in his oral presentation — that the bugs have been fixed and that the suggestions for improvement have been seriously considered.

One final note: It wouldn't hurt for the producer to personally thank the coordinator, the scribe and the various other attendees for participating in the walkthrough — after all, they've devoted a non-trivial amount of their time to help him improve the quality of his work.

Questions for Review and Discussion

1. What responsibilities does the coordinator have when the walkthrough is finished?

2. What responsibilities does the producer have when the walkthrough is over?

3. Why should the detailed comments be distributed to the participants as quickly as possible after the walkthrough is over?

4. How much time do you think the participants should be willing to spend helping the producer resolve the problems that were brought up in the walkthrough?

PART III

THE PSYCHOLOGY
OF
WALKTHROUGHS

8 OBSERVATIONS ABOUT PROGRAMMERS AND ANALYSTS

8.1 Introduction

In the previous chapters, we have discussed the *mechanics* of walkthroughs: when they are scheduled, how they are organized, and who does what to whom. So if every programmer and analyst in your organization is familiar with the rules, the roles and the procedures, all of the walkthroughs should be a smashing success, right?

Obviously not. There's more to a walkthrough than rules and procedures: A typical walkthrough involves a variety of psychological issues, many of which are only vaguely understood by the participants. This chapter and the next one are concerned with these psychological issues.

But before we begin, let's put things in the proper perspective. I am neither a psychologist, a psychiatrist nor a psychoanalyst — so any comments that I make in this chapter must be interpreted as those of an amateur observer of people who work in the data processing field. And it's unlikely that *you* are a professional psychologist or psychiatrist — so even if you did get advice from an expert in the field, you would have to interpret it and practice it in your own amateurish way. So what's the point of talking about the "psychology" of walkthroughs?

The point is very simple: Even though you may be an amateur psychiatrist, you probably have a substantial amount of experience in the data processing field — and you've probably met all kinds of programmers and analysts. By remembering what kinds of personalities you've run into during your career, you can be prepared ahead of time for many of the personality clashes that might otherwise ruin a walkthrough.

8.2 What are programmers and analysts really like?

Several years ago, I worked on a development project with a group of programmers and analysts whose personalities were almost impossible to cope with. As a group, they tended to be arrogant, opinionated, insecure and generally anti-social.* What made them behave the way they did? The only explanation that made sense to me was this: Each of the programmers had been attracted to the computer field because he preferred dealing with machines rather than people. Computers are cold, rational, deterministic things that don't talk back — whereas people are irrational, emotional, unpredictable organisms that *do* talk back.

You've probably met a few arrogant, opinionated, insecure, anti-social programmers and analysts, too. But it would be foolish to conclude that *all* programmers and analysts are arrogant so-and-so's. In fact, it's dangerous to make any generalizations about the personalities of programmers and analysts: There are now so many people in the EDP field, from so many walks of life, that one can find examples of almost *any* kind of personality.

In fact, some programmers and analysts are even nice! They're responsive, cooperative, friendly, intelligent, articulate — as well as being loyal, thrifty and brave! But they're not the ones who are going to cause trouble for you in a walkthrough. On the contrary, they're the ones who will make the walkthrough useful and fun.

It's those other people we're concerned about. Some of their more important personality traits are discussed in the sections below.

-----

* And of course I regarded myself as a humble but competent programmer who could get along with *anyone,* as long as that "anyone" was reasonable. It's virtually impossible to be unbiased when making observations about the personality of one's peers!

8.3 Programmers and analysts have a high IQ

Again, this is a generalization that does not apply to all programmers and analysts: There are some incredibly stupid people who have managed to get jobs in the EDP industry. But it is common to see at least one or two people in an EDP organization who are — or at least seem to be — geniuses. They have keen, analytical minds; they can carry out a variety of calculations in their head almost as quickly as the computer can; and they seem to have a photographic memory.

A genius programmer can be an enormous asset in a walk-through: He can spot bugs that others wouldn't find, suggest better ways of designing or coding a system and so forth. But if his intelligence is combined with a few other personality traits that will be discussed below — e.g., impatience and arrogance — the genius can be highly destructive. He can easily humiliate or insult the producer and the other participants in the walk-through; in the extreme case, the genius' verbal barbs can completely destroy the producer's sense of self-worth.

There is another aspect of the genius personality that is sometimes overlooked: their genius is often restricted to a very narrow field. Just as the *idiot savant* can multiply ten-digit numbers in his head and yet not be able to read, write or spell, so the genius programmer may be able to memorize 500-page hexadecimal dumps without being able to express his thoughts in COBOL or English. This "narrowness" is often encouraged in EDP organizations. We find data base experts, operating systems experts and teleprocessing experts who know almost nothing outside their narrow specialty.

The "specialist" genius can create havoc in a walkthrough, for his comments and criticisms often fail to take into account the "big picture." For example, the operating system expert may argue that the producer's design is wasting a substantial amount of CPU time — without appreciating that CPU time is relatively cheap and that various other factors (development time, maintainability, and the like) may be considerably more important.

How can you deal with the genius in a walkthrough? Deference and humility are probably the two best guidelines. After all, if Suzanne is ten times smarter than you, you might as well face up to it and accept her criticisms and suggestions gracefully. And there's probably no point arguing about an issue unless you're absolutely sure of yourself: Even if you're right, you may find that the genius can dazzle you with verbal pyrotechnics.

Keep in mind also that you're not supposed to argue about things in a walkthrough, regardless of whether the suggestions are made by a genius or a moron. The primary purpose of the walkthrough is to *raise* issues, not to resolve them on the spot. So let the genius make his suggestions and his criticisms without any attempt to understand them or rebut them; at your leisure, you can plod through his reasoning, and decide whether or not he's right.

8.4 Programmers and analysts are impatient, arrogant and opinionated

We could discuss each of these personality traits separately, but they are so intertwined that one often can't distinguish arrogance from impatience. Is it impatience, for example, that makes a programmer interrupt one of his fellow participants in mid-sentence to make some comment about the product being reviewed? Or is it arrogance? Is it arrogance that makes a programmer try to cut off discussion about some issue by saying, "Well, it's *intuitively* obvious that . . ." Or is it just a sign that he is highly opinionated?

As we mentioned above, these delightful personality traits are often combined with high intelligence. The genius becomes impatient when his colleagues — mere mortals that they are — are slow to understand a point he is making. He's also likely to make comments that will be interpreted by his colleagues as highly arrogant: "Well, if you knew anything about the COBOL language, you'd *know* that this statement couldn't possibly work!" And the genius often has a highly developed intuition, a "sixth sense," that enables him to spot bugs or find better solutions to a problem — but since he can't *prove* that his intuition is right, he is considered by his colleagues to be highly opinionated.

How does one deal with the arrogant, opinionated, impatient programmer or analyst? In the walkthrough itself, it's probably best not to respond to any inflammatory remarks that such a person may make — let the scribe record the his opinions, regardless of the arrogance with which they were made, and don't let an argument begin. This becomes a major responsibility of the coordinator, of course; he also has to ensure that the programmer's impatience doesn't disrupt the agenda of the walkthrough.

Outside the walkthrough, the walkthrough participants should try to explain to the programmer how they feel about his arrogance and impatience. If the participants are working together as a programming team, in the sense of Chapter 3, then they have a responsibility to resolve their personality clash — but it's obviously not the sort of thing that can be done in the middle of reviewing a HIPO diagram (nor is it the sort of thing that is likely to be resolved in one confrontation!). If the group is *not* working as a true programming team, then there are several options if the personality clash cannot be resolved. One of the most effective ones is for the producer to avoid inviting the arrogant programmer to any future walkthroughs!

8.5 Programmers and analysts are insecure and defensive

In some cases, the arrogant, opinionated programmer or analyst is merely covering up his insecurity. If he can't defend his point with rational logic, he may bluster and try to win the argument by insulting his opponent. If, as a producer, he sees that another participant is about to expose a major flaw in his product, he may begin to show extreme impatience and do everything he can to curtail the discussion (so as to minimize the embarrassment).

Note that it is the producer who is most likely to show signs of insecurity and defensiveness in a walkthrough. Why? Simply because it is his product that is being exposed to public scrutiny. The other participants can generally cover up any insecurity they feel by keeping their mouths shut — if they don't spend much time criticizing the producer's program, nobody will realize how unsure they feel about the field in which they work. But the producer has no such opportunity; and it would be normal for a person in *any* profession to be occasionally insecure about the quality of his work.

There is one aspect of the EDP profession that probably emphasizes the normal human feelings of insecurity: the speed with which today's technology becomes obsolete. A person who was both competent and confident in the 1960's now finds that he has to deal with a bewildering array of new technologies: distributed systems, data base systems, microprocessors, new programming languages, new software development methodologies, and on and on. Thus, if he proposes a technical solution to some user's information processing problem, he always has to wonder if a better solution was published in last week's *Computerworld*.

How can you deal with the insecure, defensive programmer or analyst? Since he's likely to be the producer, remember that the walkthrough is supposed to be conducted in a non-threatening, non-embarrassing fashion — so if criticisms are raised, they should be raised in the form of suggestions that the producer can think about in the (psychological) safety of his own office after the walkthrough is over. Rather than saying, "I think this program is unacceptably inefficient," a reviewer might say, "I think that the program would run ten times faster if you used Widget's Algorithm — but I'm not sure I understand the complexities of the program well enough to know whether the Widget Method would work. Perhaps you could look into it."

And if the programmer gets defensive about a criticism or suggestion, and begins to argue, remember that arguments are to be avoided in walkthroughs. The coordinator should watch for such arguments and stop them immediately.

8.6 Programmers and analysts are conservative and tradition-bound

As we mentioned above, some programmers and analysts show signs of being insecure about their work; as a result, they sometimes become defensive when presenting their product in a walkthrough. Another common consequence of this insecurity is a strong tendency to follow a *traditional* approach to solving a problem. Thus, if the programmer or analyst is accustomed to designing a business data processing system as a 1401-style sequential file system, he may continue following the same approach on a 370/168 with IMS. And if a programmer found that his COBOL compiler compiled nested IF statements incorrectly five years ago, he will continue to reject techniques like structured programming for the next ten years.

This attitude may become apparent if the programmer or analyst is a producer: The other participants will notice that he has followed an antiquated approach to solving the problem, and that he defends it vigorously. Or, if the tradition-bound programmer is reviewing someone else's work, he will typically say, "That approach won't work here — I tried it ten years ago, and it was a disaster."

How should this be handled in a walkthrough? Many of the comments made above apply in this case: Everyone, especially the coordinator, should ensure that the tradition-bound programmer does not start an argument about the virtues of the IBM 1401. At the same time, it is usually a good idea to listen carefully to what the traditionalist is saying. We *do* have a tendency in the data processing field to become fascinated with gadgets and buzzwords, and it is often useful to have someone remind us of the fundamental principles upon which all successful EDP systems are built.

8.7 Programmers and analysts are uninterested in the "real world"

As you can imagine, this is a criticism that is generally aimed at *programmers* rather than *analysts;* after all, the primary responsibility of a systems analyst is to describe the "real-world" problems that a user faces. A programmer, on the other hand, can easily insulate himself from the user and from other representatives of the real world and spend his time tinkering with hardware and software.

Indeed, "tinkering" may be an apt phrase: Many programmers play with computers as if they were toys, and approach computer programs as if they were a form of crossword puzzle. In some of the companies where I have worked, people like this were referred to as "hackers" or "code bums" — and while it may have been an unpleasant description, it fit.

What does this have to do with walkthroughs? Simply this: The "hacker" can waste a lot of time in a walkthrough arguing about esoteric features of the product which have nothing to do with the real-world requirements. And since almost *everyone* has a little bit of the "hacker" personality in him, it is easy for the entire group to begin arguing about such things as the possibility of using recursive subcoroutines to solve the user's problem.

Questions for Review and Discussion

1. Do you think that personality conflicts and other psychological issues play a major role in walkthroughs? Why?

2. On average, do you think the programmers and analysts in your organization are easy to get along with, or do their personalities make communication difficult?

3. If there are personality clashes in your organization, do you think they can be resolved by the individuals themselves? Or do walkthroughs require a resident psychiatrist to resolve problems?

4. Would you classify any of the technicians in your organization as geniuses? What are the advantages and disadvantages of having a genius participate in a walkthrough?

5. Do you think that any of the programmers or analysts in your organization are arrogant, impatient or opinionated? If so, how can you deal with them in a walkthrough?

6. Are any of the programmers or analysts in your organization insecure or defensive? How can you deal with them in a walkthrough?

7. Do any of the programmers or analysts in your organization have other personality traits that make walkthroughs difficult?

9 GAMES PROGRAMMERS PLAY

9.1 Introduction

In the previous chapter, we made a number of general observations about the personalities of programmers and analysts — and we saw that some of these character traits could have a serious impact on the effectiveness of walkthroughs. In this chapter, we address this same issue a little more directly: we consider the *games* that programmers and analysts play when in a walkthrough, and in dealing with one another outside the walkthrough.

Regardless of your position in an EDP organization — junior programmer, senior systems analyst or manager — you should have some awareness of these psychological games, so that you can deal with them when you encounter them.

9.2 The concept of games

The concept of *games* between people was popularized by Eric Berne in *Games People Play* (Ballantine Books, 1964). As Berne puts it, "A game is an ongoing series of complementary ulterior transactions progressing to a well-defined, predictable outcome." Or, more appropriately, a game is "a recurring set of transactions, often repetitious, superficially plausible, with a concealed motivation; or, more colloquially, a series of moves with a snare, or gimmick."

Games take place between people of all types — and they take place in every conceivable social situation. Berne identifies life games, marital games, party games, sexual games, underworld games, consulting room games, and even good games. Outside of the data processing profession, all of us play games with our friends, our enemies, our spouse, our neighbors and occasionally even strangers. But they take place *inside* the data processing profession, too — and that is the subject of our discussion in this chapter.

Actually, "games" have been played between one programmer and another, between a programmer and his manager, and between various others long before Berne introduced the buzzword and categorized many of the more common social games. But as we observed in the previous chapter, many programmers and analysts are basically anti-social; and by avoiding one another wherever possible, they may have avoided participating in many of the more popular games (though, as Berne points out, this anti-social behavior is often manifested in a game called "See What You Made Me Do"). In any case, the introduction of walkthroughs and programming teams has forced many programmers and analysts to deal with one another on a level that is new to them — and the games, which could previously be ignored, now become a major element in their day-to-day work.

One of the basic theses of *transactional analysis* — the analysis of interchanges which form games — is that all people operate on three different psychological "levels": a parent, an adult and a child. At one time or another, for example, each of us functions as a "parent"; that is, we respond as we remember (or perceive) that our parents responded, and we frequently use the same posture, gestures and vocabulary that they did. In other circumstances, all of us act in a childlike fashion: spontaneous, rebellious, dependent, creative and intuitive in nature. On rare occasions, all of us function as Adults: logical, rational and unbiased in our analysis of the information given to us. Since this is not a book on psychology, we will not explore these concepts any more deeply — suffice it to say that programmers and analysts exhibit Parent, Adult and Child personalities as clearly as non-EDP people.

9.3 Typical games

Berne identifies some 35 distinct games that take place between people; all of them can take place (and probably *do* take place) between programmers and analysts *outside* the office and the computer room. Many of these classical games take place *in* the office, too, and they may even take place in a walkthrough.

Since this is a book about walkthroughs, it might seem more appropriate to discuss the games that actually take place in the walkthrough itself. On the other hand, games played by the producer, the coordinator or other participants *before* the walkthrough and *after* the walkthrough can affect everyone's behavior *in* the walkthrough. So, we should discuss these games without worrying too much about where they take place in the office — it all has an impact on the interpersonal relationships in the walkthrough.

Lack of space prevents us from discussing all 35 games that Berne identifies; in addition, some games — e.g., the sexual games — have only limited relevance to our discussion of programmers and analysts in a walkthrough environment. But there are approximately eight games that I have frequently seen played in the EDP community, and they will be discussed below. For more details, and for a description of the other types of games, you should read *Games People Play* as well as Berne's other books: *Transactional Analysis in Psychotherapy* (Grove Press, 1961), and *The Structure and Dynamics of Organizations and Groups* (J.B. Lippincott, 1963).

9.4 The Alcoholic Game

The "Alcoholic Game" is, in the narrowest sense, a game played by a person with a serious drinking problem, with two to four other people. In its broadest sense, though, it describes a game involving *any* kind of "alcoholic" — that is, a person who acts as if he is "addicted" to some socially undesirable activity.

The central player in the game is the Alcoholic — the person with the problem. He interacts with the Persecutor, who berates the Alcoholic for his evil ways, and with the Rescuer, who tries to help the Alcoholic overcome his problems. There are other minor players, too: the Patsy, who unwittingly provides the Alcoholic with the means to continue his bad habits; and the Connection, who provides the direct source of supply for the Alcoholic's bad habits.

The important point here is that *all* of the players derive some psychological satisfaction from their roles — though the "satisfaction" may be simply a way of coping with other, deeper problems. The Alcoholic, for example, plays the game as a form of rebellion ("see if you can stop me"); he also uses it as a form of self-castigation, and as a way of avoiding a variety of other personal and social interchanges. The Rescuer, the Persecutor, the Patsy and the Connection all have their stake in the game, too.

What does this have to do with data processing and with the subject of walkthroughs? Well, consider the EDP variations on the "alcoholic" game: the programmer who always shows up late for work; the analyst who procrastinates and constantly fails to meet his deadlines; the programmer who continually "forgets" to attend a walkthrough; or the programmer who continually puts the same bugs into his code. The Persecutor is often the manager, though it may be one of the programmer's peers; the Rescuer, the Patsy and the Connection will typically be fellow programmers. With the introduction of walkthroughs and programming teams, it becomes easier for the Alcoholic to play his game; and it is easy for many of the walkthrough participants to fall into one of the supporting roles.

What can you do if you see the game of Alcoholic being played? It is beyond the scope of this book to provide detailed suggestions for dealing with the many ramifications of the game; indeed, even a professional therapist often has serious difficulty getting the alcoholic to stop playing his game. However, it should be possible for you to say to your colleagues, "Hey! It looks like we're playing the game of Alcoholic; and it looks like I'm the Patsy. I don't think any of us ought to be playing this game — and in any case, *I* don't want to play any more."

9.5 The game of "Now I've Got You"

The full name of this game is "Now I've Got You, You Son of a Bitch." It is characterized by Player A, who discovers that Player B has made a mistake or has somehow put himself at a disadvantage; at this point, Player A becomes much more interested in the fact that he has Player B at his mercy than he is in correcting the mistake or resolving the problem.

Walkthroughs provide an excellent opportunity for this game to take place. If the producer is presenting his code or his design, one of the reviewers may suddenly leap to his feet and shout, "Aha! Gotcha!! Look at that bug on page 13 of the listing! See, I *told* you that you didn't understand how to use nested IF's in COBOL!"

For the person playing the "Gotcha" game, there are several advantages: It provides justification for his rage (rage which may have been caused by other factors), and it avoids a recognition of his own deficiencies.

The victim of the "Gotcha" game has little choice but to respond in a low-key, calm, objective fashion: If a bug was found in his program, he should accept it as gracefully as possible. Naturally, he may wish to point out (probably outside the walkthrough) that the game is being played, and that he doesn't wish to participate. In the best of cases, the situation can be confronted, and the game can cease; in the worst of cases, the producer may decide not to invite the "Gotcha" player to subsequent walkthroughs.

9.6 The game of "See What You Made Me Do"

This game should be familiar to everyone. Most of us will admit that we've played it at one time or another in our lives. Typically, Player A is engrossed in some activity, working by himself; Player B comes on the scene, and "interrupts" Player A by asking a question or making some comment. As a result of the interruption, Player A makes a mistake — e.g., he breaks the piece of furniture he was mending, he deletes all of his files from the disk by typing the wrong command on a time-sharing terminal, and so forth. Furious with the results of his mistake, he yells at Player B, "See what you made me do!"

A somewhat more subtle form of the game takes place in the walkthrough environment. Typically, the producer will object mildly to some criticism or suggestion made by one of the reviewers, but will then accept the suggestion with a great show of diplomacy. Later on, when the reviewer's suggestion causes the producer's program to abort and waste several hours of computer time, he will yell, "See what you made me do!" Depending on the way the game is played, the producer may be trying to avoid responsibility for making decisions about his product; or he may be trying to obtain vindication for the "mistaken" suggestions that were forced on him by the reviewers.

The other participants in the walkthrough can respond in a variety of ways. They can respond to the producer's unspoken request — "Leave me alone!" — and refuse to attend any more of his walkthroughs. Or, if they think that the producer is trying to shirk his responsibility to make a difficult technical decision, they can be sure not to get stuck with the responsibility themselves.

9.7 The game of "Harried"

The programmer or analyst who plays the game of "Harried" is the one who takes on every assignment that is given to him, despite the fact that he is overworked. He accepts all of his supervisor's criticisms, yields to all of the demands made by his peers — and even asks for more. Since it is impossible for him to handle all of the assignments he has been given, he falls further and further behind and begins to make more and more mistakes.

For a variety of psychological reasons, the player may have deliberately chosen the job he is in — and he may have been attracted to his position precisely because he knew that the boss *would* continue making more and more demands on him.

Dealing with this kind of game is beyond the scope of this book, and certainly beyond the ability of most programmers or analysts in a typical EDP organization. If you see the game being played by one of your colleagues, there's not much that you can do to help other than trying to bring the situation to the attention of someone who is competent to deal with it. In the meantime, you have to be aware that the "Harried" player probably *is* taking on assignments that he can't handle, and making commitments that he can't keep. As a matter of self-defense, you will probably want to ensure that you don't become an innocent victim of the catastrophes that will eventually ensue.

9.8 The game of "If It Weren't For You"

The game of "If It Weren't For You" is normally considered a marital game. A wife will say to her husband, "If it weren't for you, I could have been a famous actress." Or the husband will say, "If it weren't for you and the kids, I could have been an astronaut." The game offers a tremendous advantage to the player: it allows him to avoid dealing with the reality that he could never have become an astronaut.

In the day-to-day humdrum of and EDP organization, "If it weren't for you" can be played in a variety of ways. Most often, it is played by the EDP manager, who complains to his staff (either singly or collectively), "If it weren't for you, we would have this project done on time, and I would be promoted to Vice President." It is rather difficult for the programmer or analyst to respond to this: about the only thing he can do is offer to quit, and the fact that the manager will eventually have to admit that he's never going to get the Vice Presidency will be a rather hollow victory for the programmer/analyst!

The game of "If it weren't for you" also takes place between peers, and the introduction of walkthroughs into the organization can easily be the source of the game. The producer, for example, may say to his fellow reviewers in the walkthrough, "If it weren't for you, I would have finished my program on time — but as it is, the boss is yelling at me because I missed my deadline." By blaming the reviewers, the producer manages to avoid facing the fact that his coding was so bad that he *never* would have made the deadline.

The simple way of responding to such a game is to say, "We're sorry if you feel that our reviews are slowing you down — perhaps you should develop your programs by yourself; we have other things to do with our time."

9.9 The game of "Look How Hard I Tried"

Many people refer to this game as the "Martyr Game." The player is usually involved in a project of some kind — a marriage, a computer program or a business project of some kind. He has already decided that the project is going to be a failure, and wants (a) to get sympathy from his peers, (b) to be perceived as helpless to prevent the failure, so that someone else will step in and take over, or (c) to be perceived as blameless for the failure.

In the data processing field, it is easy for the programmer or analyst to play "Look How Hard I Tried." He can stay at work all night long; he can sleep on the computer room floor while his program chews up computer time over the weekend. If he has a terminal at home, he can leave it logged on to the time-sharing system all night long, so that his colleagues get the impression that he has been working around the clock. And on and on.

In most cases, the game is being played between the programmer or analyst and his manager. The other programmers or analysts are typically pawns in the game and are manipulated by the player to help emphasize to the manager just how hard he was trying. Obviously, the only thing they can try to do is stay out of the game, and let the player and the manager resolve things for themselves.

9.10 The game of "Schlemiel"

The player in this game — the schlemiel — manages to make a number of mistakes, all at the expense of his victim(s). In the EDP community, the schlemiel accidentally spills coffee all over his officemate's program listing; he inadvertently deletes all of his colleague's files from the library, and so forth. The victim initially feels great anger or resentment at these "stupid" mistakes, but feels that if he shows that anger, the player will "win." So, he swallows his rage and smiles at the schlemiel; when the schlemiel apologizes, the victim — if he follows the rules of the game — offers forgiveness. The game continues, often over a period of days or weeks: The schlemiel continues to make mistakes, until finally the victim is no longer able to contain his rage.

How does one deal with this? In a sense, the victim can't win: If he shows anger at the first incident, the schlemiel will feel justified in returning the resentment. If he swallows his anger, the game will continue indefinitely. The best approach is the direct one, and one that most victims find difficult to put into practice. The victim might say, for example, "Wow, you really *are* a schlemiel! I guess I'd better change my file access password so you don't destroy any more of my files. And it's really a pain in the neck to have you spilling coffee on my listings — maybe I should talk to the boss about getting our office assignments changed."

9.11 The game of "Yes-But"

The last game we'll discuss is one that comes up often in a walkthrough environment. The player begins the game by stating a problem; for example, "I don't see any way of coding this part of the program without using nested IF statements — but our standards say that we're not allowed to use nested IF's." One of the other participants responds by offering a solution — e.g., "Why don't you solve the problem by using decision tables?"

Unfortunately, every solution that is offered is rejected with a "Yes, but . . ." comment by the player. For example, "Yes, but our decision table preprocessor generates terribly inefficient code." And if another participant offers a different suggestion, it too will be rejected. Thus, if he says, 'Well, why don't you code the program with ELSE-IF constructs instead of nested IF's?"

the response will be, "Yes, but that kind of code looks ugly."
And so it goes.

Eventually, it becomes obvious that *no* solution will be accepted. The way to get out of this game is to say to the player, "Yes, it *does* seem to be a difficult problem! How do you propose to solve it?"

9.12 Summary

We have looked briefly at only a few of the more common games that take place between people. In certain social situations — e.g., parties — the games become "pastimes" and may be a pleasant way of whiling away the time. In a situation like a walkthrough, though, the games usually interfere with the business at hand — and they may lead to a complete breakdown of communication between the various participants.

The primary thing we have attempted to do in this chapter is to make data processing people aware that such games *do* exist; prior to the introduction of walkthroughs, they may not have been forced into sufficiently close contact with their colleagues to have to face the reality of games. As we have seen in many of the examples, the best solution is usually to avoid getting sucked into the game.

Questions for Review and Discussion

1. Can you think of examples of each type of game that we have talked about in this chapter? Discuss them with your colleagues and see whether you all agree as to the proper way of dealing with the game.

2. Can you think of additional types of games that take place in your walkthroughs? If so, consult *Games People Play* to see whether it is a "standard" game.

3. Do you agree that the best way of dealing with most of the games is to refuse to participate? Are there any other solutions that you can see?

PART IV

MANAGEMENT'S ROLE
IN
WALKTHROUGHS

10 CONVINCING MANAGEMENT WALKTHROUGHS PAY OFF

10.1 Introduction

In some organizations, data processing managers are unconvinced that walkthroughs are a cost-effective way of doing business. "What a waste of time," they say. "letting a bunch of programmers sit around a table and argue about their programs."

Or, the manager will say, "Why not let the computer find all those bugs? After all, we have a time-sharing system — so the programmers can find their own bugs at a terminal! Isn't that why we got a time-sharing system in the first place?"

There is often some validity to these comments. And even if there weren't, many managers would *think* that there was. So it's something that needs to be discussed. Are walkthroughs *really* cost-effective? In all cases? Can the cost-effectiveness be demonstrated? Is it tangible? Or does the manager have to rely on some "gut feeling" that the *intangible* benefits of walkthroughs make them worthwhile?

It has been our experience — and the experience of the majority of our friends, our colleagues and the clients with whom we work — that walkthroughs *are* worthwhile, and that their benefits *can* be measured in tangible terms in most cases. The purpose of this chapter is to discuss the benefits of walkthroughs from a management viewpoint, so that management *can* be convinced that the investment in walkthroughs is worth the effort.

10.2 The economics of bugs

We should begin by emphasizing again that one of the major purposes of a walkthrough — if not *the* major purpose — is to find errors or "bugs" in a product. From a management viewpoint, the question should be: Can bugs be found more economically in a walkthrough environment than in the "classical" environment? Since the classical environment usually requires the producer to find his own bugs prior to a formal review, the real question is: Is it more economical to let the producer find his own bugs, or is it better to let a group of 3-5 people find the bugs?

The honest answer is: It depends. If the producer is a genius who never makes mistakes, a walkthrough is almost certain to be a waste of time and money. On the other hand, if the producer is an idiot who can barely spell his name without making a mistake, walkthroughs are worth their weight in gold (metaphorically speaking!). The problem is that most producers are neither idiots nor geniuses (nor are the reviewers who participate in the walkthrough), so it is not intuitively obvious how the manager can eliminate bugs in the most cost-effective manner.

One of the primary factors in this "cost-benefit" calculation is the *turnaround time* for fixing errors: This is particularly evident when we are talking about walkthroughs of code. If the programmer is using a typical batch computer system for program development, he will often have to wait several hours for his program to be compiled or for a test run to be completed; indeed, overnight turnaround is the norm in many organizations.

And what does the programmer do in the meantime? Whether the manager wants to admit it or not, the answer quite often is: *nothing*. Of course, the programmer will *look* busy — after all, it's not considered proper for the programmer to have his feet up on his desk, drinking a can of beer and reading *Playboy*. However, it's likely that he will be involved in "busywork" that serves very little purpose.

Sometimes the programmer *does* have other things to do — other modules to code and the like. However, there is still a certain amount of time lost whenever he has to mentally switch gears from one task to another. In addition, it often takes 10-15 minutes to put away one set of program listings, HIPO diagrams or other documents, and make room on one's desk for another set.

What does all of this have to do with walkthroughs? One of the objectives of a walkthrough is to ensure that the product is correct the *first* time. Thus, if the walkthrough is successful, a program should only have to be compiled *once;* it should only have to be tested *once.* *

To illustrate this, let's take a specific example. I recently had an opportunity to participate in a walkthrough with three programmers in a small programming shop. The four of us spent approximately 45 minutes reviewing roughly 200 lines of PL/I code. The investment of three person-hours paid off handsomely: We found a total of 25 bugs. It's particularly interesting to see what *kind* of bugs they were:

- approximately 5 bugs were syntax errors

- approximately 5-10 bugs were trivial logic errors

- approximately 5-10 bugs were moderately complex logic errors

- approximately 5 bugs were "impossible" logic errors

Why 5 syntax errors? The reason is simple: The walkthrough was conducted immediately after the program had been written on a coding pad — *before* it was keypunched, and *before* it was compiled. As we first observed in Chapter 2, walkthroughs

---

* That is, the program should only have to be tested once (with oodles of test cases) to see whether it works by itself. One would expect to see the program tested several more times in a "system testing" environment.

are usually not conducted at this early stage — the producer's writing was hard to read, and the coding sheets had been reproduced on an ancient copier that produced nearly illegible copies on a waxy paper that looked suspiciously like the toilet paper one finds in English restrooms.

It was not much fun reading the program under those conditions. Nevertheless, it was probably cost-effective to find those 5 syntax errors — even though the PL/I compiler would have found them in a matter of milliseconds. The problem was that the organization had overnight turnaround for compilations, so a day would have been wasted while the programmer fixed the syntax errors and resubmitted the program for compilation. And, of course, there's no guarantee that she would have fixed those errors without introducing a few new ones.

As for the logic errors, it is absolutely certain that the walkthrough was more cost-effective than allowing the producer to find them by herself. Several of the bugs were trivial and would have been exposed with any kind of test data. Nevertheless, they would have required at least one recompilation of the program — so at least one more day would have been lost. Indeed, it's much more likely that *several* recompilations would have been necessary: The producer was the sort of programmer who would typically find only one bug with every test run.

Several of the bugs would have been even more expensive had the walkthrough not found them first. It would have been evident to the producer that something was wrong (e.g., the program would have blown up, or it would have produced gibberish output) but it would not have been intuitively obvious *what* was wrong. Left to her own devices, the producer would have used program dumps, traces and other debugging techniques to isolate the bugs. All of which is time-consuming and expensive — not only in terms of the producer's time, but also in terms of the computer time, printer paper and computer operator's time.

Finally, there were the "impossible" bugs — some 5 or 10 situations which *never* would have been found by the producer. Since the program was written in an organization that was too small to have a separate Quality Assurance Department or Testing Department, it follows that these bugs would have remained in the code until after it was put into production. A friend of mine calls these bugs "time bombs," and the description is an apt one!

Most walkthroughs don't produce results quite as dramatic as the example described above; it is more common to find 3 or 4 errors in a walkthrough. Even so, this means that the program can be compiled, tested and made ready for further system testing in one fell swoop — and the programmer doesn't waste several days waiting to get the bugs out of his code.

The payoff tends to be even greater when bugs are found in design walkthroughs and specification walkthroughs. Some recent studies indicate that it is roughly ten times less expensive to fix design errors that are detected in the design phase of the project than it is to fix them after the code has been written.* In practical terms, this means that a product that has had walkthroughs in the earlier stages of development can be expected to go into production without the usual last-minute problems and crises one often expects to see in a project.

Having said all of this, let's mention some situations where the walkthrough might *not* be so cost-effective:

1. If the programmers have access to a time-sharing system with fast response time — and if the development project is not directly charged for the time-sharing services it uses — then some of the arguments above might not be as valid. Even so, the computer will only "find" the bugs that the producer is clever enough to expose with properly chosen test cases; and debugging, even in a time-sharing environment, can be a time-consuming process. In such an environment, we suggest that the walkthrough take place *after* the program has been compiled but *before* the producer has spent any time doing his own testing. Note that the same comment applies to design

---

* See Barry Boehm, "Software Engineering," *IEEE Transactions on Software Engineering,* December 1976.

walkthroughs and specification walkthroughs: If the producer has access to a large staff of artists, typists and other administrative support with which to produce a specification or design document quickly, then a walkthrough should take place after a *legible* document has been produced.

2.   If the producer is known to be a near-genius who makes almost no mistakes, the walkthrough may not be necessary. *Very* few managers would be willing to bet their next paycheck that their analysts and programmers would be able to produce a complex system without errors — but one does occasionally run into "simple" projects that might be produced in an error-free manner by an average analyst or programmer.

3.   If the *cost* of a bug is small enough, a walkthrough may not be cost-effective. It has been traditional in many organizations to let the users find the bugs in a computer system *after* the system is put into production — presumably because the organization could *afford* to let them find the bugs. In most of today's large, complex systems, we can no longer afford to do business this way: A bug in a large on-line system, for example, often costs the organization thousands or even tens of thousands of dollars. But, as a manager, you may wish to evaluate the cost of discovering a bug in a production system versus the cost of discovering it in a walkthrough.

10.3 The psychology of finding bugs

In many discussions about walkthroughs, there is an assumption that the producer *could* find the bugs in his program or his design if he were given enough time. But in the discussion above, we mentioned the concept of "impossible" bugs — bugs that the producer would *never* find regardless of his efforts.

Why should this be so? It's very simple when you think about it: In looking for errors in his product, the producer is likely to make the same logical errors that he made when he built the product in the first place. If, for example, a programmer forgot to check for an exceptional condition in his code, then he'll probably forget to invent a test case which will cause the exceptional condition to occur.

Many managers argue that the problem is even more fundamental: The producer has no psychological motivation to invent test cases that will demonstrate that his product is *wrong*. Instead, he is motivated to demonstrate that his product *works!* One can see this attitude among programmers quite often: They treat their programs like a fragile piece of china and will provide only those test cases that are sure not to upset the delicate mechanisms within the code. Given this state of affairs, it is not so surprising that a number of bugs will remain undiscovered if the testing is done exclusively by the producer.

10.4 Intangible benefits of walkthroughs

In Chapter 1 we pointed out three "intangible" benefits of walkthroughs:

- improved *quality* of the product

- training, and exchange of technical information among the programmers and analysts who participate in the walkthrough

- insurance: a greater probability that the product can be salvaged if the producer leaves the project before he is finished

How much are these benefits worth? In the final analysis, only the data processing manager can tell. All we can do in this book is state that the majority of EDP managers with whom we have talked have confirmed that the walkthroughs *did* improve the quality of their product, that they *did* increase the level of

technical expertise on the part of the staff, and that they *did* eliminate the need for scrapping partially completed products.

There is one other reason for the manager to introduce
walkthroughs into his organization: They make day-to-day work
more fun for most programmers and analysts. There are some
cases, of course, where programmers and analysts complain that
walkthroughs are *not* fun (a problem which we'll discuss in section 10.6 below), but most agree that it's much more fun to
work in an environment where problems, excitements,
discoveries and all of life's day-to-day trivia can be shared with
one's peers. In simple terms, many managers have reported that
morale and the general "spirit" of their staff has increased
significantly as a result of walkthroughs.

10.5 Situations where walkthroughs may not be justified

As we have already pointed out, there may be some situations when an EDP manager cannot cost-justify a walkthrough.
If the producer develops high-quality, error-free products or if
the cost incurred by a bug is small, there may not be much incentive to subject the product to a walkthrough. Since the walkthrough probably costs \$50-\$100 (i.e., 1-2 hours of time invested
by 3-5 people whose salary, with overhead, probably averages
\$10 per hour), the manager has to ask himself whether he can
expect to get \$50-\$100 in benefits.

There are one or two common cases where a manager may
feel that it is particularly difficult to justify a walkthrough. One
such case is the "one-person" project: a project worked on by a
single producer for a relatively short period of time. It often
turns out that the other programmers or analysts in the organization are working on entirely different projects (e.g., other one-
person projects), so no one can be expected to have any familiarity with the producer's product. In addition to the normal investment of time required by the walkthrough, the manager has
to ask himself whether it is worth spending the time allowing the
producer to familiarize his fellow programmers and analysts with
the general nature of the application on which he is working.
This might well require another hour or two, and may even in-

volve specialized knowledge that the other programmer/analysts could not be expected to have. We have seen this situation primarily in *small* data processing organizations; e.g., a scientific data processing organization where the programmers write relatively small FORTRAN programs for engineers, chemists, physicists and other scientists, or a business data processing group where the programmers produce relatively simple report-writing programs for managers in other parts of the company. If indeed each programmer and analyst is working on distinctly different applications, then it may not make sense to require them to walk through each other's products. However, the situation is usually not so extreme: The applications are often rather similar (after all, a report-writing program is a report-writing program regardless of the details), and it often takes only a few minutes to familiarize someone with the general nature of one's product.

There's one other consideration to keep in mind: Very few one-person projects that *remain* one-person projects forever. Sooner or later, the producer moves on to bigger and better things — and his computer system is turned over to someone else. Without a walkthrough approach, there's a good chance that the product will be relatively unintelligible to the maintenance programmer.

Speaking of maintenance, we should ask another management-oriented question: Does it make sense to have walkthroughs in a maintenance environment? Once again it's a question of trade-offs. If the maintenance activities involve making one-line changes in small programs, and if the cost of a mistake is small, then there's no urgent need to insist on walkthroughs. On the other hand, if the product is large (e.g., a system containing several hundred programs and several hundred thousand lines of code), a walkthrough is likely to have all of the benefits that we have discussed throughout this book — *especially* if the original product was developed in an "unstructured" fashion several years ago. What appears to the maintenance programmer to be an innocent change to such a "rat's-nest" system may have subtle ramifications throughout other parts of the system. Walkthroughs thus have the advantage of minimizing the nasty surprises that make maintenance programming such a pain in the neck.

In some maintenance organizations, walkthroughs have come about for a different reason: the staff is too small to assign each programmer his own "personal" program to maintain. One of our clients, for example, has a staff of three programmers who maintain some five hundred different programs. Most of these programs work very well — which is lucky, since the three programmers couldn't possibly manage five hundred "buggy" programs. The only problem is that they don't know *which* program is likely to cause them trouble at any point; or, to put it another way, they don't know which of their programs will require modifications and enhancements to suit the whim of a user. And, of course, it's impossible to remember the details of five hundred different programs over a long period of time, especially if you look at them only once or twice a year. Consequently, the three programmers tend to work as a team: If a program has to be changed, all three programmers will look at the listing, discuss the change and walk through the modified code. The whole process may only occupy them for an hour or two — after which they go on to the next program to be modified.

There is one last situation where the manager may have to abandon the idea of walkthroughs: if his project gets seriously behind schedule. There is an old saying that applies to EDP development projects as well as a number of other things in life: "People never seem to have time to do a job right the first time, but they always have time to do it twice." Unfortunately, this is often true of EDP projects that were originally estimated to take one year but then stretch into two years. Pressure from impatient users and frustrated managers means systems are designed hastily, coded sloppily and tested inadequately. And we can now add an item to that list. Such projects find that their walkthroughs get done hurriedly, without adequate preparation — or not all.

10.6 What can go wrong with a walkthrough?

So far, we have talked about problems that might prevent a walkthrough from being held — but we have implied that once a walkthrough begins, it will be successful. Obviously there are no guarantees that this will be the case. As we observed in Chapter

6, walkthroughs are *not* some kind of magic ritual that causes bugs to rise out of the paper and smack the reviewers on the nose. It is quite possible that the programmers and analysts will fall sound asleep in the walkthrough, and that nothing will happen at all. Thus the manager must ask: What can go wrong in the walkthrough? How can the problems be prevented?

The major problems, in our experience, have been:

- The participants "goof off" and begin discussing things that have nothing to do with the product being reviewed.

- The participants become involved in long arguments about minor — if not trivial — points; arguments about the "style" of the product are especially common.

- The participants become involved in personality clashes which obscure the real subject of the walkthrough.

These problems, if not properly controlled, can render the walkthrough useless. Indeed, it can be even worse: The participants can become embroiled in such bitter arguments that they may stop speaking to one another.

How can these problems be avoided? Well, the first thing the manager must do is ask himself whether the following assumptions are valid about the people who participate in the walkthroughs:

1. they are inexperienced in the procedures and mechanics of the walkthrough

2. they are human, and are thus prone to lapse into discussions of irrelevant subjects even though they know they shouldn't

3.   they are inexperienced at giving or taking criticism so they may have trouble discussing bugs or weaknesses in the product without making someone lose his temper

4.   on the other hand, they basically respect the intelligence, competence and integrity of the other participants

5.   they feel a sense of responsibility for making the product succeed within the given constraints — e.g., schedule, budget and so forth.

If assumptions 1, 2 and 3 are incorrect, then the participants have very little excuse for wasting time or conducting an unsuccessful walkthrough. On the other hand, if assumptions 4 or 5 are incorrect, there is almost no point in holding the walkthrough: It is almost guaranteed to fail.

This last point is a serious one, especially if the participants in the walkthrough are chosen arbitrarily (e.g., according to some corporate standards) or if the participants are chosen by an amateur (e.g., the producer himself, who may not appreciate the human dynamics of the situation). Thus, the most important thing that the manager can do is ensure that the participants *do* respect one another, and that they *do* feel a sense of responsibility for the success and quality of the product.

Once this has been done, there are several specific suggestions that we can make for overcoming the problems listed above:

1.   *Be prepared to let the participants waste some time.* Remember that they aren't experienced in the mechanics of walkthroughs, so the first one or two walkthroughs may be an utter waste of time. Be prepared to walk past the conference room where the walkthrough is being held and hear raucous laughter, shrieks and giggles, and all the other evidence of a drunken orgy.

2. *Rely on the group's sense of responsibility.* After one or two unproductive walkthroughs, the participants will almost always begin worrying about their lack of progress — *if* they have a sense of responsibility towards the product. Thus, if they get into the same argument that they got into on the *previous* walkthrough, one of the participants is likely to say, "Hey, we got into this argument last time — I'm getting bored with this!" A compromise reached this way is *much* more effective than if the manager forces a compromise down their throats.

3. *Enforce the 30-60 minute time limit.* One of the primary reasons for chaos in a walkthrough is that the coordinator allows the discussion to get out of hand. Typically, this means that the walkthrough drags on for an hour or two, with the participants arguing the same points over and over. While the manager should *not* take over the coordinator's role in the walkthrough (see Chapter 11 for more details on this), he can often help impose discipline by strictly enforcing the 30-60 minute time limit. If the participants know that they have to be finished and out of the conference room at the end of an hour, they will tend to stop their bickering soon enough to get some work done.

4. *Insist that the participants sign the walkthrough report.* As we discussed in previous chapters, the standard walkthrough procedure requires the participants to sign the walkthrough report after voting on the status of the product. Some participants think this is a formality and will conveniently "forget" to do so; the coordinator may also be lax in asking the participants to sign the report. From the manager's point of view, though, getting the signatures is important — for it emphasizes to the participants that they *are* responsible for the outcome of the product. One manager friend of mine solved his problems with walkthroughs by insisting that the walkthrough report be signed and then filing the report for easy reference. If any of the

computer systems aborted in the middle of the night in a production run, he would then call *all* of the participants into the computer room to fix the bug!

5.   *Make sure that the participants have some standards for programming, design or analysis.* As we have mentioned, many of the arguments that take place in a walkthrough concern the "style" of the product. These arguments can be reduced, though probably not eliminated, by ensuring that the participants have a set of standards with which they can all agree. In some cases, the standards will be a subset of the corporate standards; in other cases, the group may want to adopt a superset — e.g., stricter than the "normal" standards. In any case, the manager may well find that the first few walkthroughs in a new development project will concern the standards by which the group agrees to design and code. Once this is accomplished, subsequent walkthroughs should run much more smoothly.

Questions for Review and Discussion

1. Do the managers in your organization generally feel that walkthroughs are cost-effective and worthwhile? If not, what kind of arguments could be used to convince them?

2. As an experiment, try to estimate the average cost of a walkthrough by computing the average salary of the participants, plus any overhead costs that may be involved. Then try to estimate the number of bugs that will be found in the walkthrough and the savings that are likely to result — i.e., estimate how much money would have been spent finding the bugs in the "classical" fashion. Can you demonstrate the effectiveness of walkthroughs in this manner?

3. What is the average turnaround time for compiling and testing programs in your organization? What do the programmers *really* do while they're waiting ?

4. How many bugs would you expect to find in a typical walkthrough?

5. If you have access to a fast-response time-sharing system, do you think walkthroughs are worthwhile?

6. Do you agree that producers find it psychologically difficult to find their own bugs? Can you cite any evidence of this in your own organization?

7. Are walkthroughs worthwhile in an organization heavily oriented towards "one-person" projects? What are your reasons?

8. Are walkthroughs worthwhile in a maintenance environment? Why (or why not)? Is the situation fundamentally different from a development environment?

9. What should a manager do if he finds that the participants in a walkthrough are "goofing off" and not devoting their attention to the subject of the walkthrough?

10. What should the manager do if he finds that certain partici-
     pants have serious personality clashes with one another?

11. Do you agree that the manager should allow the partici-
     pants to "waste" the first one or two walkthroughs? What
     are your reasons?

12. Why is it important that the participants be asked to sign
     the walkthrough report?

11 AVOIDING THE URGE TO ATTEND WALKTHROUGHS

11.1 Introduction

Throughout this book, we have advised that managers *not* participate in walkthroughs conducted by their subordinates. However, we have only hinted at the reasons for this advice — and while some people may feel the reasons are obvious, others may be thoroughly puzzled. Hence this chapter, whose purpose is to explore the issue more deeply.

We will begin by discussing the reasons that a typical programmer or analyst feels intimidated by the presence of a manager in a walkthrough. Then we will examine some of the typical reasons that a manager *wants* to participate in a walkthrough. We will see that in most cases, the manager can accomplish the sort of things that he needs to accomplish without interfering with the normal walkthrough process.

11.2 Why should managers avoid walkthroughs?

The primary reason for suggesting that managers should avoid walkthroughs is that it interferes with a frank, open exchange of views between peers. Regardless of what the manager actually *does* in the walkthrough, his mere presence is usually perceived as a signal that the *producer,* rather than the product, is going to be evaluated. As one programmer told me, "Every time the boss attends the walkthrough, I start worrying that he's keeping score in his little black book — and at the end of the year, he's going to tell me that I'm not getting a raise because I had a total of 378 bugs during the year." Even if the manager is not keeping score, it's difficult to avoid the normal human reactions when bugs are observed in the product: The producer feels a combination of fear, humiliation and inadequacy, while the manager feels a combination of condescension and impatience.

If the producer sincerely feels this way, it is difficult for him to avoid playing a variety of games in the walkthrough; in many cases, the participants respond with their own games. The producer, for example, will tend to defend his product against the criticisms and suggestions made by the participants: In the extreme case, what they perceive as a bug in his product, he will regard as a "feature" of the product. When the reviewers suggest improvements to the style or organization of the product, the producer is likely to proclaim immediately that the changes are "not possible," or that they're "stupid." Of course, the producer *should* be accepting such suggestions without comments and then deciding *after* the walkthrough how to deal with the suggestions. But nobody wants to make a fool of himself in front of his boss — so the producer will tend to get into arguments *in* the walkthrough, which means that the coordinator will have a difficult time maintaining his role.

Meanwhile, the participants may have their own games to play. If they don't think highly of the product, what better forum for voicing their displeasure than in front of the boss? More importantly, if they don't get along well with the producer, the reviewers will tend to be more than normally critical of the product. They, too, will begin to argue over issues of style — when they *should* be simply stating their criticisms and moving on to the next point.

All of this can take place even though the manager sits quietly in a corner of the room. In many cases, the manager is unwilling or unable to play such a passive role: He, too, begins looking for bugs in the product and begins arguing about its style. And since he *is* the boss, the other participants (not to mention the producer and the coordinator) are somewhat obliged to let the manager have his way. In effect, the manager ends up running the walkthrough — and since he is likely to have a stronger personality than the participants, he ends up dominating the walkthrough.

In some organizations, simple peer-group reviews have evolved (or degenerated, depending on your point of view) into reviews organized by, and run by, the manager; indeed, the reviews often take place in the boss's office, just so no one will forget who is in charge. If the participants — including the manager — are honest, sincere, egoless people with no ax to grind, such a review can run smoothly. In most organizations, however, one of two things will generally happen: (a) the review will degenerate into a shouting match, or (b) the participants will perceive that it's best for them to keep their mouths shut and let the manager do whatever he wants to do.

Some managers don't believe all of this. "I get along perfectly well with my programmers and analysts," they say. "My presence doesn't affect them at all in the walkthrough — after all, we're adults, not children!" We've noticed that such a manager rarely asks his programmers what *they* think about his presence; and if he does ask, the question is often posed in such a way as to make it obvious to the programmers that they should not object to their manager's presence! And if such a manager participates in a walkthrough, he's likely to find (that is, if he looks!) that (a) he has become a player in the game played between the producer and the participants, or (b) the games are indeed being played, but they have been repressed for the sake of social etiquette (which is, in itself, a complex game!). Or, he may find that the programmers and analysts are not arguing with each other simply because they've abdicated responsibility for the product.

There is one case where it often *does* make sense for a manager to participate in a walkthrough: If the manager also functions as a programmer or analyst, then his products will presumably be reviewed along with everyone else's. This usually happens when the manager is a team leader, or lead analyst, or senior programmer — i.e., a first-level manager who has responsibility for the day-to-day activities of a few subordinates, but who generally does not have authority to hire, fire or grant salary increases. And since such a person is usually a "player-coach" who is producing as much technical work as his subordinates, his presence in the walkthrough is almost unavoidable. Nevertheless, such a manager should be aware that he will still be perceived by the other programmers or analysts as a "boss." Even if *he* can't determine the amount of their raise, they worry that he will pass negative recommendations up to the next level of management. We will suggest a way out of this dilemma in the next section.

11.3 Why do managers want to attend walkthroughs?

Having pointed out the problems caused by the manager's presence in a walkthrough, we should ask: Why would a manager want to attend a walkthrough anyway? When we understand the reasons, we can usually suggest a way of satisfying the manager's legitimate needs without destroying the walkthrough concept.

Though he may not admit it, one reason that a manager may want to attend a walkthrough is curiosity. He may simply wonder what goes on in a walkthrough. What do the programmers do to one another? Is it really worthwhile? What he would really like is an opportunity to watch the participants in a walkthrough through a one-way mirror; failing that, the manager will sometimes insist on attending one or two walkthroughs, just to satisfy his curiosity.

If this is the case, the participants can often satisfy the manager's needs by arranging a "demonstration" walkthrough. Depending on the situation, the participants may want to select a product that is known to be in reasonably good shape (i.e., one that will probably not have any embarrassing bugs); or they may want to select a product that was developed by someone who is no longer with the organization (a program that is already in production may be a good choice). In some cases, it may be interesting to walk through a product developed by the manager back in the days when he was a technician — but watch out for the obvious political problems!

In most cases, the manager will only want to sit through one or two such walkthroughs — so it needn't be too much of a strain for the participants. Eventually, the manager will discover that he really doesn't understand the subject matter being reviewed; or he'll get bored listening to discussions about detailed technical issues; or he'll decide that he has better things to do than attending a walkthrough!

Why else would a manager attend a walkthrough? Some managers insist on attending the walkthrough because they are convinced that the participants will "goof off" or become involved in endless technical arguments. In blunt terms, the managers don't trust the participants to conduct an effective walkthrough.

In Chapter 10, we discussed a number of ways of avoiding the dangers of arguments among the participants, "goofing off" and walkthroughs that stray off the subject. In most cases, these problems *can* be overcome by the manager — but, as we pointed out, it may take time, and the manager should be prepared to "waste" the first few walkthroughs. If the manager is convinced, though, that the participants will *never* be able to conduct themselves properly in a walkthrough, then he might as well abandon the walkthrough approach completely and substitute a formal review in its place. In such a case, it would probably be better to have a one-on-one review between the manager and the producer — not a pleasant prospect, but probably better than having a roomful of squabbling technicians arguing over trivia.

There is yet another situation where the manager may feel strongly that his presence in the walkthrough is required: if he has considerably more technical knowledge and experience than the producer or any of the other participants. This may happen, for example, if the manager has several years of programming and systems analysis experience, while his staff consists primarily of junior programmers. Naturally, the manager is nervous that the producer and the participants may overlook serious bugs or may not be aware of sophisticated solutions to the problem.

The solution? Let the manager attend the *second* walkthrough. In other words, let the producer and the participants have a walkthrough by themselves first — they'll find many of the "stupid" errors that they wouldn't want the manager to see. Once they're satisfied with the product, then the manager can conduct a more formal review — just as a Quality Assurance Department may insist on its own review after the walkthrough has taken place.

There remains one reason for the manager to participate in the walkthrough: He may be a technician himself. As we mentioned above, many organizations have "player-coaches" who write programs and also supervise the day-to-day activities of other programmers. It is inevitable in such circumstances that the manager will participate in the walkthroughs of his subordinates; all he can do is minimize the political "games" that we warned about at the beginning of this chapter. One way of doing this is to ensure that the manager is properly humble about walkthroughs of *his* products: If the other programmers and analysts see that the manager makes mistakes and is able to accept criticism, then they are likely to be somewhat more willing to do the same themselves.

Unfortunately, this won't eliminate all of the problems. The manager should expect that his subordinates will continue to be nervous about his presence in the walkthroughs for several months — nearly six months in one organization I visited. Only after they have survived one or two salary reviews is a typical programmer or analyst likely to *really* believe that management is not keeping a count of the number of bugs in his program.

Questions for Review and Discussion

1. Is it standard practice in your organization for managers to attend walkthroughs?

2. Do you agree that a manager's presence is likely to make the producer feel nervous and defensive? Will the programmers and analysts openly admit that they feel this way?

3. What kind of games have you seen producers play when a manager attends one of their walkthroughs?

4. What kind of games have you seen managers play when they attend walkthroughs?

5. What can the producer and participants do if the manager *insists* on attending the walkthrough? What do you think of the idea of having a semi-secret "private" walkthrough that the manager doesn't know about (the local bar is often a good place for this)?

6. Why do *you* think that managers want to attend walkthroughs? Are their reasons legitimate?

7. What can be done if the manager is simply curious to see how a walkthrough operates? Does the idea of a "demonstration" walkthrough make sense in your organization?

8. If the manager is also a producer (i.e., he writes code or is responsible for part of the design of the system), do you think it is OK for him to attend the walkthroughs of his subordinates? What problems is this likely to cause? What can be done to avoid these problems?

12 PERFORMANCE EVALUATION IN WALKTHROUGHS

12.1 Introduction

Whenever managers discuss the concept of walkthroughs and team programming, one question invariably comes up: How can we evaluate the performance of the people who participate in the walkthrough? How can the "good guys" be rewarded? And how can the "dummies" be identified? As we have pointed out in previous chapters, managers are discouraged from attending the walkthrough — so they don't know how many bugs were found, how many idiotic programming techniques were used by the producer, or who came up with the brilliant way of solving the problem.

Surprisingly, many programmers and analysts feel the same way. "Why should I carry that clod?" they'll argue. "The only reason his program works is that I found all the bugs! And my programs always pass the walkthrough the first time — with no bugs!" Naturally, all of this tends to be intimately connected with promotions, raises and other forms of reward and recognition.

So, it's a problem that both managers and technicians worry about. We will begin this chapter by examining the "current" situation in more detail — i.e., how do managers evaluate the performance of their technicians in a non-walkthrough environment? We will then discuss the impact of walkthroughs on the process of performance evaluation.

12.2 Comments on "classical" performance evaluation

In most of the organizations I have visited (not to mention the ones I've worked in!), programmers, analysts and other technicians are reviewed once or twice a year. The reviews range from informal chats with one's immediate supervisor to highly formalized rituals, complete with appropriate forms, and attended by two or three levels of management. The result may be a promotion, a raise or a pat on the back if things have gone well; or a rebuke, a demotion or dismissal if things have not gone well.

It's difficult to say whether the average performance review is fair, or accurate, or "honest." And it's difficult to make generalizations about the methods by which managers arrive at their decisions. But there do seem to be some common characteristics to these reviews, and they are particularly interesting in the context of walkthroughs.

For example, I've noticed that *technical competence* is only a small factor in many performance reviews. When I was a junior programmer, I assumed that I would get a larger raise at the end of the year if my code was efficient, if my programs were well-documented and if my projects were completed on schedule. And if my programs were three times more efficient than Charlie's and I finished my program three times faster than Charlie, then naturally I'd get three times larger a salary increase than Charlie. I soon learned that that wasn't necessarily so!

Of course, things are more extreme in some organizations than they are in others. In one large bank I visited in Montreal, the programmers and analysts spent quite a lot of time arguing about the technical virtues that were most likely to give them a large salary increase — until one programmer summed it up rather neatly by saying, "In the final analysis, it doesn't matter what kind of programs we write. If a program should take one month to develop, and we take two months, nobody notices. And if it should run in 100K bytes of memory, and we gobble up 200K bytes, nobody cares — and if they *do* care, they'll just buy more memory, or use virtual memory."

"All they really care about," this programmer went on to say about her managers, "is that we show up for work on time, that we wear respectable clothes, that we work quietly at our desks, and — most of all — that we not do anything to upset the users outside the EDP department."

Sounds pretty grim, doesn't it? Yet it may be more accurate than many of us would like to admit. In this modern age, we rarely see the lone programmer toiling away in the computer room, single-handedly accomplishing technical miracles; it may have been true in the 1950's and 1960's, and it may make good drama on television, but it doesn't reflect the reality of modern life in a data processing department.

Whether we like it or not, most EDP departments *are* bureaucracies. They consist of dozens — if not hundreds — of people working on complex projects for other departments whose motivations they don't understand. Modern data processing is intimately involved with human bureaucracies, human systems and human politics — and the people who excel in modern data processing are those who, *in addition to a requisite minimum knowledge of the technical details,* are talented at dealing with people.

In other words, if you are a programmer, it *does* matter whether you wear a clean shirt to work. It *does* matter whether you take a bath more than once a week. It *does* matter whether you show up for work on time. And it *does* matter whether you can get along with your fellow programmers and analysts, as well as the manager and the users. And in a large majority of organizations, all of this matters *much* more than the speed of your code or the extent of your familiarity with IMS, OS or the IBM System/370.

To the extent that technical competence *is* important, we have to ask: How well can a manager judge the technical ability of his subordinates? Most managers will admit that this is an extremely difficult thing to do, and that it may be impossible. After all, each programmer or analyst works on a different assignment — and each technician will argue that *his* project is more difficult than anyone else's, and that it may be the most difficult project the world has ever seen. And since we have no well-defined metric with which to measure the complexity of a computer system,* we almost have to take their word for it.

Of course, a manager with a great deal of experience may be able to use the following argument:

1. One of my subordinates, Fred, spent the last 12 months working on a FOO program which barely works and which doesn't seem to completely satisfy the user's requirements.

2. When I was a junior programmer working on the IBM 1401, I developed a FOO program in one month — and it's been running without any bugs since then.

3. Two or three other programmers that have worked for me during the past several years have managed to write a FOO program in two to six months without any major difficulties.

4. Ergo: Fred must not be such a good programmer.

The trouble with all of this is that it's usually a false comparison — an attempt to compare apples and oranges. For example:

1. It probably took the manager three months to develop his version of the FOO program many years ago (everyone, including Fred and the manager, would prefer to forget about those "fuzzy" periods of systems analysis and the tedium of testing, and remember instead the brilliant few days of coding).

2. In the days of the IBM 1401, the user probably didn't expect his FOO program to do as much. And he was likely to be far less critical of what he got.

3. In the days of the IBM 1401, the manager probably didn't have to document his program. Fred, on the other hand, has to fill out ten pages of forms,

---

* This may be changing: See *Elements of Software Science,* by Maurice Halstead (Elsevier, 1977).

specifications and status reports for every page of code he writes.

4.   The IBM 1401 *worked*. The modern-day Kludgevac 807 probably doesn't. And neither does the fancy data base management system Fred is supposed to use.

5.   On top of everything else, Fred is supposed to be using structured programming and structured design on his FOO program. But since he doesn't *know* structured programming and structured design, he's learning as he goes.

6.   The boss conveniently forgets that Fred is maintaining three other systems while he works on his FOO program.

7.   And in the final analysis, the reason that the boss *is* the boss is that he *is* better than Fred — or at least is able to convince everyone else that he's better.

We could go on, of course — but the point should be clear. A manager can use his own personal experience, his observations of other programmers and analysts, and his "gut" feelings to determine whether Fred has been doing a good job. But all he can *really* do is identify the high and low ends of the spectrum: the extremely good and the extremely bad technicians.*

And, in the final analysis, does it really matter? In more and more organizations, workers expect and receive near-automatic salary increases (sometimes euphemistically referred to as a "merit" raise, as opposed to a "cost-of-living increase") regardless of whether their performance was 10 percent above or below average. Only the people at the high and low ends of the spectrum merit special attention. The extremely talented technician is given a 20 percent salary increase instead of the usual 10 percent — even if his performance was 10 times above average.

---

* This assumes, of course, that the manager *does* have some technical knowledge and experience. Some managers don't — e.g., they may be ex-accountants who have been asked to take over the EDP department.

And the extremely incompetent technician is:

(a) given a 5 percent salary increase — after all, we don't want to hurt his feelings!

or

(b) given *no* salary increase — maybe he'll take the hint and quit in another year or two.

or

(c) transferred to the maintenance department.

or

(d) fired — an option that is used, quite literally, as a last resort in most large EDP organizations.

12.3 The impact of walkthroughs on performance evaluation

The main point of the preceding discussion was to put the subject of performance evaluation in some perspective. It is appropriate to ask how technicians are evaluated in a conventional organization, and then to ask how that process will be impacted by walkthroughs.

Let's begin with a simple observation. Since a technician's performance is based largely on non-technical criteria, walkthroughs should have no impact on the evaluation process. After all, management can still determine whether their programmers show up for work on time, whether their analysts interact well with the users and so forth.

But is it as simple as that? The walkthrough approach *does* introduce a major change in the social dynamics of the EDP organization: The programmer or analyst is expected to attend walkthroughs, participate in the review of other people's programs, and accept constructive criticism of his own programs. Thus, the manager may wish to include the following questions in his review of the technician:

1. Did he generally make himself available for walk-throughs or did he refuse to participate? Did he insist on being a loner — and if so, did he produce enough to justify such anti-social behavior?

2. If he accepted an invitation to a walkthrough could he be counted on to attend — or did some last-minute crisis frequently prevent his attendance?

3. Did he invest the necessary time and energy to study the programs and designs of other technicians in the organization — or did he do a superficial job of preparation?

4. Did he generally follow the procedures for walk-throughs in Chapters 4, 5 and 6?

5. Was he able to give and receive criticism easily — and did he concentrate on criticizing the *product* rather than the *producer?*

Of course, many of these questions will be difficult for the manager to answer — simply because the manager is not present in the walkthrough, and thus cannot judge first-hand what the technician is doing. In any case, it does seem that the walk-through approach may "hide" certain information from the manager regarding the programmer's technical competence. However, just because the walkthrough takes place behind a closed door does not necessarily mean that it functions as a black box. In the organizations where I have worked, the manager was still able to identify the people at the high and low end of the spectrum. The manager could not easily tell which of his "average" people were better than the other "average" people — but he probably couldn't tell before walkthroughs were introduced.

Why is it that the manager can identify the very good and the very bad people? Part of it has to do with productivity: While walkthroughs generally improve *everyone's* productivity, it is still true that the talented programmers and analysts will produce considerably more than the dummies in the organization.*

In addition, the normal office gossip will make it very clear who the talented technicians are, and who the incompetents are. If Charlie requires 17 walkthroughs before his program is approved, the manager will certainly hear about it; indeed, the other programmers and analysts may refuse to participate in the walkthroughs if they feel they are "carrying" Charlie.† At the same time, the manager will hear about the walkthrough in which Mary's program is praised by everyone for its documentation, its elegance and its efficiency. In other words, the hero who single-handedly saves the project with his brilliant work won't be made invisible because of the walkthrough; and the dummy will find that the walkthrough doesn't hide his incompetence from the rest of the world.

As for the others, the manager has to accept the fact that he will lose some information on which to judge the technical competence of his people. But things tend to average out. If Fred finds two bugs in Mary's program on Monday, there's a good chance that Mary will find two or three bugs in Fred's program on Tuesday. And if that's the case, why should the manager care whether Fred had more bugs than Mary?

Keep in mind also that the manager can always ask to look at Fred's program outside the walkthrough. Fred's program will reflect some of the suggestions, improvements and criticisms of the various reviewers, but it will probably still show a lot of Fred's personal handicraft.

---

* A classical study indicated that some programmers could finish their projects 28 times faster than others, and that their program would be 10 times more efficient than the programs written by others. See "Exploratory Experimental Studies Comparing Online and Offline Programming Performance," by H. Sackman, W.J. Erickson, and E.E. Grant, *Communications of the ACM*, January 1968, pp. 3-11.

† Some people have suggested that the programmer's performance could be judged by the number of walkthroughs required to produce an "approved" product. This may be OK for extreme cases (like 17 walkthroughs), but is probably dangerous if the manager tries to establish a threshold of 2-3 walkthroughs as a measure of competence. If the reviewers know that this is Charlie's third walkthrough, they may be more inclined to approve the product, even though it is still inferior — and, naturally, Charlie will not be in a mood to accept constructive criticism.

There is one last comment to make about the impact of walkthroughs: sometimes it provides *more* information to the manager than the classical approach, and thereby helps deal with a phenomenon that my colleague Tim Lister calls the "living legend." Consider the case of Veteran Vic, who has been with the organization for 20 years. Vic played a major role in developing the financial reporting system, which runs 6 hours a day, and consumes 2 megabytes of memory and 43 spindles of disk storage. And during the first two years of production, when the system was extremely shaky, Vic spent many long nights in the computer room — fixing bugs, rerunning jobs, writing "quick-and-dirty" programs to recreate clobbered master files, and the like. Having been around so long, Vic has now acquired the title of Senior Software Systems Analyst; he's a "living legend," and the other programmers and analysts treat him with the deference that the title requires.

But has anyone seen any of Vic's code lately? Does anyone know whether Vic *can* code? In fact, does anyone know whether the financial reporting system was developed *because* of Vic, or *in spite of* Vic? Many of these questions can be answered if Vic is requested to subject his programs to a walkthrough. In some cases, Veteran Vic will truly be recognized as a veteran — and the junior programmers and analysts will have an opportunity to learn from a master of the trade. In other cases, Vic will have a hard time maintaining his stature, his title or even his job. I have seen one or two veteran programmers resign — with a great deal of righteous indignation — rather than be subjected to the indignities of a walkthrough.

To summarize, the manager may find that he loses a little information because of the "secrecy" of a walkthrough; on the other hand, it opens up the systems development process and exposes the living legends who might otherwise have escaped detection. Walkthroughs do *not* destroy the manager's ability to detect extremely talented and extremely untalented people; nor do they interfere with the manager's ability to judge non-technical aspects of the technician's performance.

Questions for Review and Discussion

1. How often do performance reviews take place in your organization? Does a performance review always take place at the same time as a salary review? Is it the general opinion of the programmers and analysts in your organization that the review is fair?

2. What are the major factors in the evaluation of a technician in your organization? How many of these factors are technical, and how many are non-technical?

3. How accurately do you think a manager can judge the technical competence of his subordinates? By what methods does he rank their technical abilities?

4. Does your organization provide different salary increases for *every* technician, or does it place each technician in one of three or four categories — e.g., "good," "bad" and "average"? If the technician is placed into categories, is it generally true that everyone who falls into the same category gets the same salary increase?

5. If walkthroughs are introduced into your organization, will a technician's performance be judged partly on the basis of his willingness and ability to participate in walkthroughs?

6. Do you think that a manager will be able to identify *very* talented people and *very* "untalented" people in a walkthrough environment? How?

7. Do you have any "living legends" in your organization? Will walkthroughs help expose their talents, or lack of talents, for everyone to see?

13 BUILDING TEAMS

13.1 Introduction

In Chapter 3, we introduced the concept of *programming teams.* We pointed out that many organizations are unwilling or unable to form true programming teams, but that they *can* implement the concept of walkthroughs — even if they have a conventional project organization.

Regardless of whether your EDP organization plans to organize "true" programming teams, any attempt to implement walkthroughs necessarily involves a certain degree of teamwork. After all, everyone in the walkthrough has to agree to a certain set of rules and procedures; and everyone has to agree that their purpose is to review the *product* rather than the *producer.*

But is it likely that your organization will actually develop the type of programming teams described in Chapter 3? Is it likely that EDP management will be willing to assign a project to a team, and then let them manage their day-to-day activities completely? As you might imagine, the concept seems very radical to many organizations — almost communistic! In such organizations, the concept of programming teams is either entirely abandoned or the teams function in an "underground" sense. That is, the programmers and analysts know that they're working as a team, and perhaps even the first level of management knows — but all of the members of the team continue carrying out their normal day-to-day activities so that the "normal" management hierarchy will not think that anything has changed.

We will not be discussing strategies of underground revolutions in this chapter, nor will we be discussing organizational guerrilla warfare; instead, we will assume that you, as a manager, are interested in forming programming teams within the normal framework of your organization. Since this is not a management textbook per se, our discussion will be limited to a series of suggestions for successful formation of programming teams within your organization.

13.2 Guidelines for forming teams

Obviously, the main ingredient in forming programming teams is a commitment on the part of a manager: While "underground" teams *can* form spontaneously among the programmers and analysts, a host of political problems make it difficult for them to continue their existence. So, to begin with, you must *want* programming teams to form and flourish; if you are ambivalent, it's probably better not to bother with the idea.

The second ingredient — though it's not absolutely necessary — is a project for the team to work on. Once the "team" concept catches on, you'll find that it doesn't have to be project-oriented: a team could be working on three or four small project simultaneously. But in the beginning, a single project gives everyone — team members and outside managers — something to focus on. So, if you're trying to form a programming team, wait until you have a development project of about the right size and then assign it to the team.

With these two basic groundrules, most EDP organizations simply form a team assign them a project, and then "play it by ear" — i.e., deal with any unusual situations as they arise. In most cases, the team begins to show a personality of its own after a few months, and both management and the team members will learn how to deal with the new environment. In most organizations, neither the programmers, the analysts nor the managers can claim to be expert psychologists, so everyone has to blunder along with their amateur understanding of the social dynamics — but they *do* manage to get along.

With this in mind, you may find the following suggestions helpful in building programming teams:

1. *Let teams evolve naturally.* Many organizations form their first programming teams by taking a group of people who were already assigned to work on a project, and simply telling them that they are now part of a new social organization. Only later does management realize that two of the team-members violently dislike one another, and that two others argue incessantly about abstract programming issues — and by the time this is discovered, the team may be on the verge of collapse. The moral: you can't create teams by an arbitrary decree. The fact that five or six people have been working together on the same project is obviously some indication that they can communicate with one another; however, you should talk privately with each individual to see whether personality problems or other issues may prevent them from functioning as a true team.

2. *Don't disband the team at the end of the project.* As we have mentioned, many organizations form their first teams around a specific development project. At the end of the project, it is natural for management to reassign the programmer/analysts to other projects, thus effectively destroying the team. Since it is a rather delicate matter determining which technicians can work well together, and since it usually takes a few months for even the best of friends to learn how to work together in a team, it seems a shame to waste that investment of time and energy by destroying the team at the end of the project. Why not let the team stay together, and simply assign it a new project?

3. *Encourage fresh blood in the team.* The major problem with the suggestion above is that a group of programmer/analysts may become technically stale after working together for a few years — that is, they get themselves into a rut, and keep using the same kind of approach for every new project, even when

the situation calls for fresh, new approaches. In addition, people often get bored with one another after working together for five years! For these reasons, it's very healthy to allow — and even encourage — some turnover of people in the team. This will usually happen without any overt actions on the part of management: One team member will leave to take a better job in another company, another may leave because his or her family is moving to East Podunk, and so forth. The new programmer or analyst who joins the team brings his own experiences and his own perspective, which will be assimilated into the collective experiences of the team. As Gerald Weinberg says, "Programmers come and go; the team abides."

4. *Respect and trust the team.* This seems like an obvious piece of advice: After all, *without* trust and respect it is impossible for the team to function. Nevertheless, it is common for many EDP managers to display mild distrust of the team's day-to-day activities and to begin dabbling in its affairs. It is perfectly proper for management to ask the team to establish periodic checkpoints and milestones (e.g., on a weekly or monthly basis, depending on the size and nature of the project) and to ask for a full accounting of progress at each "checkpoint meeting." But if it looks like the project is getting a little behind schedule, or if it appears that two team members are spending a lot of time arguing with each other, the manager should resist his first impulse to step in and solve things himself. If necessary, the entire team can be gathered together and confronted with the problem (or management's perception of the problem); such occasional "showdown" meetings allow the team to maintain its own integrity, and still give management the satisfaction of seeing the problem openly aired and resolved.

5. *Reward and punish the team equally.* In some cases, the team members themselves may suggest to management that one of their members has done an

outstanding job, and that he or she deserves special recognition. This rarely happens, though — and the manager is courting disaster if he tries to make his own decision about the relative contributions of each team member. As we pointed out in Chapter 12, performance evaluation is often based on non-technical factors; thus, it is possible that a manager *could* decide that team member A deserves a larger salary increase than team member B without ever having to decide whether A's programs are better than B's programs. However, this is likely to introduce an element of competition among the team members, which will make it more difficult for them to function effectively as a team. So, unless it is absolutely impossible, we advise that you reward (or punish) the team members equally.

6.   *Protect the team from outside pressures.* In a typical organization, a programming team will be an "alien" unit within the bureaucracy. One of the most useful things that the manager can do is protect his team members from the meetings, the memos, the forms and the administrative procedures which would otherwise consume their time, their energy and their patience.

Questions for Review and Discussion

1. If programming teams are not officially endorsed by your organization, do you think they could function on a "sub rosa" basis? Could this be done by the programmers and analysts themselves, or would it require active participation on the part of first-level managers?

2. How can you tell whether a group of programmers and analysts are likely to be able to work together as a team? Will *they* know? What kind of questions can you ask them to determine whether the individuals are compatible?

3. In your organization, are programmers and analysts normally reassigned at the end of a development project? Is it possible for them to continue working together on a new project?

4. Do you feel that members of a programming team should be rewarded or punished equally? Why (or why not)?

BIBLIOGRAPHY

Berne, Eric, *Games People Play* (Ballantine Books, 1964).

I personally consider this to be the most interesting and most relevant of Berne's works. It introduces and defines, in clear terms, the concept of a game; and it contains dozens of descriptions of games that we all encounter in everyday life.

—. *The Structure and Dynamics of Organizations and Groups* (J.B. Lippincott, 1963).

I first read this book while preparing the manuscript for *Structured Design,* based on the recommendation of my coauthor and friend Larry Constantine; we have both found it a useful pedagogical technique to draw analogies between hierarchies of modules in a software system and hierarchies of managers in a human system. This book by Berne is extremely interesting in this context, and it further extends the concept of games and transactions.

—. *Transactional Analysis in Psychotherapy* (Grove Press, 1961).

This book is for those who wish a more thorough treatment of the concept of "transactions" between human beings. Some of the writing goes beyond what the average layman is likely to want to know, and possibly beyond what he is likely to understand.

Boehm, Barry, "Software Engineering," *IEEE Transactions on Software Engineering,* December 1976.

This excellent survey does not mention walkthroughs, but it does an excellent job of describing the many problems in software development — problems that walkthroughs can often help alleviate. One of the most useful aspects of Boehm's paper is the effort to *quantify* the cost of bugs, and the cost of other problems in the software field; the other useful aspect of the paper is the extraordinarily extensive bibliography.

DeMarco, Tom, *Structured Analysis and System Specification* (YOURDON inc., 1978).

Too many people associate "bugs" with errors in the code; in many cases, a bug is an indication of an error in the design phase — i.e., the programmer faithfully coded an incorrect design. Even worse, a bug can be caused by a flaw in *analysis.* It is becoming more and more apparent that the flaws in systems analysis are caused by two major factors: (a) our inability to document the requirements of a system in terms that are readily understandable to both user and analyst, and (b) our grim determination to build the *entire* system before we give the user a chance to indicate whether he likes it. DeMarco's book addresses both of these problems: He describes a process of top-down implementation that allows the user to see "skeleton" versions of a system before it is too late to rectify mistakes. And he discusses a number of graphic techniques — data flow diagrams, data dictionaries, and Structured English — with which to bridge the communications gap between user and analyst. I consider this book essential reading for any systems analyst.

Fagan, Michael E., "Design and code inspections to reduce errors in program development," *IBM Systems Journal,* Vol. 15, No. 3, (July 1976), pp. 182-211.

> Fagan is one of the chief exponents of the formal "inspection" — a form of walkthrough in which there is a predetermined list of program features that must be addressed in the walkthrough. For certain types of production programming, this approach has had extremely good results; Fagan's paper is a must for those who intend to make walkthroughs a way of life in their organization.

Halstead, Maurice, *Elements of Software Science* (Elsevier Press, 1977).

> I think Halstead has made a valuable contribution to a field that is often characterized as an "advanced state of witchcraft." He has developed a model with which one can describe the complexity — in *human* terms — of a program (or a module in a larger system). The preliminary efforts to validate the model seem highly promising; these include analyses of several of the Collected Algorithms of the ACM, as well as "real-world" programs developed within such industrial organizations as General Motors. If Halstead's model is eventually accepted, it will become considerably easier for programming managers to compare the complexity of the tasks they have given their programmers.

Jones, T. Capers, "Measuring programming quality and productivity," *IBM Systems Journal,* Vol. 17, No. 1 (January 1978), pp. 39-63.

> Most discussions about programm*ing* and programm*ers* involve the abstract concept of *quality* and the presumably more tangible concept of *productivity.* However, we have learned that it is almost as hard to

measure productivity as it is to measure quality —
certainly it has become clear that "lines of code per
person per day" is a dangerous measure. Mr. Jones's
article is a thoughtful survey of the criteria that
managers have used to measure both productivity and
quality — and though it won't answer all of our questions, it certainly helps clarify some issues.

Kernighan, B.W. and P.J. Plauger, *The Elements of Programming
Style* (McGraw-Hill, 1974).

Many code reviews degenerate into trivial arguments
because the reviewers disagree about the *style* with
which the code was written. Kernighan and Plauger's
book is an excellent source of ideas on the various aspects of programming style. I would recommend that
this book be read before a programming team tries to
develop its own standards; the book and a brief set of
standards should help minimize most arguments over
style in a code review.

Lewis, Paul, "Group, Not Line, Builds Sewing Machines," *New
York Times,* March 18, 1978.

The concept of programming teams has often been
compared to production teams in other industries —
most often, the automobile industry. This article in
the *New York Times* gives yet another example of a
production team in Karlruhe, West Germany. Instead
of automobiles, these workers make sewing machines
— but is there all that much difference between sewing machines, automobiles and computer programs?

Sackman, H., W.J. Erickson, and E.E. Grant, "Exploratory Experimental Studies Comparing Online and Offline Programming
Performance," *Communications of the ACM,* January 1968, pp.
3-11.

This paper is considered *the* classic in the area of comparing the performance of programmers. The fundamental problem most managers have is that their people are all working on different problems — but in the Sackman experiment, they were all working on the *same* program. Even though the paper is a decade old, the results are still very much worth reading.

Walston, C.E. and C.P. Felix, "A method of programming measurement and estimation," *IBM Systems Journal,* Vol. 16, No. 1 (January 1977), pp. 54-73.

This paper provides extensive and reasonably objective measurements of a variety of the disciplines mentioned in this book: structured programming, structured design, librarians, top-down development and even structured walkthroughs. *Must* reading for those trying to measure the impact of the new software development methodologies.

Willoughby, Theodore C., *Proceedings of the fifteenth annual computer personnel research conference* (Association for Computing Machinery, New York, 1977).

The Special Interest Group on Computer Personnel Research (ACM/SIGCPR) regularly considers a number of issues in the training, evaluation, hiring, care and feeding of programmers. Recently, though, they have been increasingly interested in the subject of teams; the proceedings of this conference are particularly interesting in this respect. I note with some pride that the proceedings include a paper by our very own Tom Plum, describing the results of six months of walkthroughs in our own company.

Weinberg, Gerald M., *The Psychology of Computer Programming* (Van Nostrand, 1971).

> This is the granddaddy of all books and articles on walkthroughs, team programming and a number of related issues. Almost everyone who reads the book is likely to say, "Yeah, I did that, and I thought that, and I kinda knew about all of those things . . ." But Weinberg was the first to *write* about them, and the result is, in my opinion, *must* reading for everyone in the computer field — managers and programmers alike. Precisely because it *is* such a classic now, it is ironic that several reputable publishers declined to publish the book when the manuscript was first presented to them. The reason? Simple: At the time, there weren't any university courses on the psychology of computer programming — so it was obvious that the book wouldn't sell!

Yourdon, E. and L.L. Constantine, *Structured Design,* 2nd edition (YOURDON Press, 1978).

> Throughout our discussion of walkthroughs, I've mentioned the concept of structure charts, HIPO, data flow diagrams and other aspects of *structured design.* This book discusses such concepts, and may be a useful reference for those engaging in design reviews.

—. *Techniques of Program Structure and Design* (Prentice-Hall, 1975).

> As we have pointed out in our discussion of walkthroughs, it is difficult to conduct a walkthrough of code if the code is poorly structured, disorganized, and riddled with cryptic data names. *Structured programming* is often suggested as a good discipline for developing clear, readable code; this book discusses

structured concepts and the broader question of programming *style*, and may be a useful reference for
those conducting code reviews.

INDEX